THE WEEKLY GAME PLAN

The Ultimate Guide for Creating YOUR Best Year

BY

SCOTT FICHTER

Ordering Information: Quantity sales. Special discounts are available on quantity purchases by corporations, associations, and others. Orders by U.S. trade bookstores and wholesalers.

DREAMSTARTERS

www.DreamStartersPublishing.com

TABLE OF CONTENTS

Dedication

This book is dedicated to my beautiful wife, Stephanie,

and two wonderful children, Aubrie and Aiden,

for always believing in me.

I love you three so much!

Heart, Star, Crown!

Gratitude First

Every day I start by giving thanks and displaying gratitude to God for the blessings he has given me. So I thought, what better way to start out this book than to give gratitude to God and others who I am so grateful for in my life.

To God:

Thank you for your commitment to me, Lord. Thank you for your belief in me every day. Thank you for sending your son to die for my sins. Thank you for instilling me with values. Thank you for always being there, 24/7, to pray in times of either happiness, sadness, pain, sorrow, or celebration. Thank you for the many blessings you have given me in my life. Thank you for the opportunity to share my experiences and impact someone else's life!

To my wife:

Stephanie, you are the backbone of our family and our relationship. You are such a strong woman and a positive influence on me and our children! Thank you for being the amazing woman you are and always supporting me! I am so blessed to have you as my wife and my best friend.. Being able to spend my life with you and being on these amazing and fun journeys with you is just awesome! I love you!

To my kids:

Aubrie and Aiden you are wonderful! You are my inspiration to be the best that I can be. You are the most precious gifts in life I could have ever received! You and mommy are a huge part of my 'WHY'! I am thankful for you every day and I love you more than you will ever know! Heart, Star, Crown!

To DreamStarters Publishing:

Mike Fallat, a true friend from high school, thank you for supporting me through the book writing and publishing process! I appreciate your drive for success and how you have helped me and others be a part of a special tribe and grow our circle with some great people!

To everyone who I have crossed paths with in life:

Thank you to every single person I have ever encountered in my life. If we met for a minute, spoke one time, you are a friend or family member, a business acquaintance, a restaurant server, or anyone I have interacted with ever, thank you! I appreciate you being a part of my life in some form and a part of my development into the person I am today. May God bless all of you in your life's journey!

Foreword

Now and then you come across a book title and think, here we go again with another game plan that MAY or MAY NOT work FOR ME... but not this time!

I was never a huge fan of a book that is written about another person's life experiences and how I can mold my own life from what I am reading. When my husband said that he was going to write a book, I said *"About what? Who is going to listen to you?"* In 2018, he wrote down short and long term goals on a whiteboard in my home office with a green marker that read: *"3-5 years: Write and publish 2-3 books."* I had to stare at this for the last three years waiting patiently to see when this was going to be done and if it was ever going to happen. The funny thing is that I experienced first-hand the take action game plan and daily logs that Scott went through to get this on print to help others - all of YOU who are going to embark on the same experience. How exciting is that?!?

Well here we are, three years later, Scott with his first book and I couldn't be more proud! He didn't write this book until he changed himself first. He went through 52 weeks of this exact plan that you're about to embark on. It won't be easy each week and it might change your mindset a lot, but know that this is the type of book that you don't have to wait until the end to find out who you are or what you want to do to better yourself. It's a journey that will take you on a wild ride of your own life and I KNOW for the BETTER!

The Weekly Game Plan is a simple read, yet a thoughtful plan on how to change you – whatever that may be. It's perfect for that busy mom, single person who needs to find their purpose, a multi-job dad, or the couple in their early 60's who just want to find their purpose again and reconnect. Week by week, it will let your mind think, grow, and accomplish what you really want and how to get there! Don't let the football game plan pictures fool you – Scott does have a plan for you that works. Enjoy your first week to the last. Do this for YOU, you won't regret it!

Stephanie Fichter M.B.A, PHR and KCS Certified
Change Management Leader

Introduction

"Our failures don't define us. How we respond to those failures is our true definition."

Regional Finals!!! A shot to go to Nationals! A team that unexpectedly won their conference, set a school record, and now has a shot at school history! This is their moment, this is their time! The flags are raised up! All zones are clear, ready to go!

The official calls all competitors to the start, *"Runners, take your mark."* The runners enter their blocks, prepared for the race of their life.

The official says, *"SET!"* There is a brief pause, then...

BANG!

The gun goes off and the first leg of the 4x100 meter relay is underway. Around the first turn they come! The underdog conference champion in the lead.

Approaching Exchange Zone 1. The second runner begins to take off. The first runner, with a small lead yells, *"STICK!"* Runner 1 reaches out the baton, but oh no, Runner 2 drops it! NO!!!

The baton is dropped and has crossed over lanes. The Cinderella Story is over as the team is officially disqualified! The dream of going to Nationals shattered as the first time all year this team has dropped the baton.

Tears shed, previous accomplishments overshadowed by this moment. A moment that would change and shape the next 10 years of Runner 2's life. PAIN! FAILURE!

THE WEEKLY GAME PLAN

Ladies and gentlemen, I was Runner 2. Sports were my life. I measured everything about me and my life based on my accomplishments and performance in sports.

Sure, I had made mistakes before: Struck out, missed a tackle, threw an interception, but this was one I could not rebound from like the others.

I couldn't say, *"I'll get them next play, trust me."* No. This was it. Worst of all. After all of the championships, trophies, and awards, this was my final moment in my competitive sports history. A failure that cost my team a medal and a chance to go to Nationals.

This moment lived in the back of my mind and haunted me internally for a decade. An entire ten years of my life, this one failure played a HUGE part in affecting me, my mindset, my confidence, and my COMMITMENT to going for my goals again.

I know it should not have affected me the way it did, but with my life being all about sports and working towards becoming a professional athlete, this was devastating.

PAIN that would live with me in the back of my mind until 2017, when I was able to admit to my wife and a new friend Isaac in Sacramento, how this had affected me. It was at that moment when I finally talked about it that I could finally forgive myself and move on.

You see, we all have moments of failure, moments that break us. It's not these moments that define us, but how we grow and respond to them that does. How we stay **COMMITTED** to our goals!

Every one of you reading this book. You are the reason I wrote it. I believe in you. I believe that you can overcome any failure. You don't need to be broken for days, weeks, months, or years like I was. You just need a GAME PLAN to get your mind back on track.

This broken mindset led to failed interviews, failed friendships, failed tryouts, and a failed mentality. When I recommitted myself, and stayed COMMITTED until the end goal of success, that's when I landed my first teaching job, I bought a brand new car, I met my wife, I worked towards my Master's Degree, and I had two (2) wonderful children.

During this time of success did I encounter other failures? Absolutely. The difference was that I learned how to overcome them. I relearned COMMITMENT.

As we start on this journey, my challenge for you is COMMITMENT. Let's be COMMITTED together to get you where you want to be! Whether that's in your personal life, work life, school life, business life... let's get there!

I believe in you!!!

Coach Scott Fichter L.B.S. M.Ed.
Certified Life Coach | Entrepreneur | Football Coach | Professional Speaker
Co-Owner of S2A Legacy, LLC
Creator of Coach Fic's Football Academy
#noslackjusthustle

WEEK 1 GAME PLAN:
Motivating Your Journey

#noslackjusthustle

"No Slack Just Hustle!"

Wooooo! How is everyone feeling? Are you excited? It is a blessing, honor, and a privilege to be writing this book and helping to motivate your journey! My vision is to help you for 52 weeks, 365 days, by motivating your life's journey to make a difference and positive impact!

I have hopes of inspiring you, being real with you, and letting you know anyone can go through a struggle in life and have a shot at coming out again on top to leave a legacy. It's not the struggle itself that defines who we are, but it is the response to that struggle that molds our character and makes us into what we truly can be: CHAMPIONS!

My goal is for you to feel as if we are having a conversation with each other and to get that energy across to you. I am passionate about helping others, and hope you see and feel that passion throughout this year-long journey too.

What are your passions? What are your dreams? Not sure? That's okay. Let's help you find them!

My suggestion is to read this book in the exact order it has been laid out as I have organized each week for a specific purpose! At the end of each week's reading is a ***Question for Thought, a Take Action Game Plan Journal Entry, and a Daily Log***. These are very important because they provide you an opportunity to journal your thoughts. You can also join our group on social media: ***No Slack, Just Hustle*** to be a part of the conversation, discuss how your journey is going, and so much more!

Remember, this is about you! I want you to succeed, I want you to experience greatness, and I want you to be a champion.

So are you ready? Are you ready to get started?

Let's change some lives on this journey! It may be yours, it may be someone you know, and it may even be mine again! That's exciting!

You are all great, you are all champions, and you can achieve many things!

It's time! It's time! It's time to go get your dreams! Let's motivate your journey!!!

Question for Thought

What motivates you to be successful?

Week 1 Take Action Game Plan Journal Entry

Write your top three (3) things that motivate you to want to be successful. Provide 1 reason for each of them:

Reason 1:

Reason 2:

Reason 3:

Daily Log

Write down what motivated you each day to start working towards your goals:

Day 1:

Day 2:

Day 3:

Day 4:

Day 5:

Day 6:

Day 7: *Rest and Reflect Day (You will understand in Week 6 why! Be patient, do not read ahead.)*

WEEK 2 GAME PLAN:
The Legacy Mission

#noslackjusthustle

"Success is a Decision"

So you want to change your life, your home, your school, your business, your community, the world?

First, it starts with changing you.

Everybody wants to see change. But the key to change is taking action and doing something about it. A legacy mission is to impact the world, impact your family, impact your business, impact your school, or impact your community in a positive way so that each person you work with is empowered with the ability to also leave a legacy that is lasting, positive, and effective.

Every day is an opportunity to make a difference in someone's life, which can be so powerful and affect an exponential amount of people without us ever knowing. One person truly can make a difference and begin changing the world.

Maybe you heard some of these phrases before: You're not good enough! You can't do it! You won't make it! Maybe you even heard these from family and friends. These phrases. These phrases mean nothing! They don't control you. They don't control your outcomes. Others don't control you. Only you control you! Realize that first!

It's your time! It's your time to start changing those phrases from negative to positive. It's your time NOW! Erase the negativity and start replacing it with your own positivity.

Repeat after me and yell it for everyone to hear: I am good enough! I will do it! I will make it! For I. I am Successful!

The key to success is always continuing to be willing to learn, grow, and plant seeds in others to build a positive and promising future. Let's work together and make a difference, why? Because together, we can truly impact the world!

Question for Thought

What is something you can do today to make a difference in someone's life?

Week 2 Take Action Game Plan Journal Entry

Write three (3) ways you can do something positive for yourself and/or someone else to make a positive impact:

Way 1:

Way 2:

Way 3:

Daily Log

Write down what you did each day to make a difference in someone's life. (Remember it doesn't always have to be something big or extravagant, the little things matter!):

Day 1:

Day 2:

Day 3:

Day 4:

Day 5:

Day 6:

Day 7: *Rest and Reflect Day (You will understand in Week 6 why! Be patient, do not read ahead.)*

WEEK 3 GAME PLAN:
Finding Inspiration

#noslackjusthustle

"Find what inspires you, then begin inspiring others!"

10:27 PM: The couple looks on as their new born child is being weighed by the nurse. The couple smiled at each other with overwhelming joy!

They were told they would never have kids, and to great surprise, they now have a beautiful baby girl weighing 7 pounds, 3 ounces. Both parents inspired more than ever to help people to continue to have faith that true miracles can happen!

What an amazing story of inspiration!

Inspiration... It's all around us. It could be like what the couple had recently experienced, or maybe it's something different for you.

What inspires you? Is it your Family? Nature? Wildlife? Something else?

Inspiration is everywhere, but the feeling of inspiration... The feeling of inspiration is inside of you.

Inspiration comes from within. It comes from an overwhelming feeling of joy when you see what it is that inspires you.

Today... Go! Go find what inspires you! Find your inspiration!

Then... use that inspiration. Use it to do amazing things!

Question for Thought

What inspires you to be great in everything you do?

Week 3 Take Action Game Plan Journal Entry

Write down the top three (3) things that inspire you:

Inspiration 1:

Inspiration 2:

Inspiration 3:

Daily Log

Write down how you will use the inspirations you have everyday to remain positive and push towards your goals:

Day 1:

Day 2:

Day 3:

Day 4:

Day 5:

Day 6:

Day 7: *Rest and Reflect Day (You will understand in Week 6 why! Be patient, do not read ahead.)*

WEEK 4 GAME PLAN:
The 3-6-5 Commitment

#noslackjusthustle

"The 365 Commitment"

6:00 AM: The alarm goes off, Joe turns over, hits the snooze button to sleep for 5 more minutes.

7:30 AM: The alarm goes off, Joe turns over, looks at the time, and wakes up in shock!

On January 1, Joe set goals that he was going to be committed to for this year. His goal was to wake up everyday at 6:00 AM to read a personal development book, exercise, and eat a healthy breakfast. This was the third day in a row he missed his time!

How many times has this happened to you? We start off the year all gung ho that we will meet our goals for this year. Then 90 days in, 60 days in, 30 days in, or even less than a week in, we fail.

Our response: *I'll get 'em next year.*

Well, that mindset is now gone. If we fail, then the next day we come back again and work for success!

You see, right now, we have reached the point that the entire book is focused on! I strategically made you wait until week 4 to provide you with this information. Our focus is on a 365 day, 52 week, **GAME PLAN** of being committed to you. It is the number of days/weeks in a year, and the number of days/weeks that you have an opportunity in that year to develop yourself and make greatness happen in your life!

Think about that for a moment, 365 daily opportunities to impact your life, or to make a difference in as many lives as possible over a 52 week timeframe.

Can you be dedicated to making that commitment to yourself? To your personal development? To helping others?

The decision is yours to make, but my challenge to you is this: Take this **GAME PLAN** seriously! Are you up for that challenge? Odds are against you as most people quit things within the first 90 days. Will you commit to 365 days/52 weeks for yourself? I believe in you! I believe you can!

Question for Thought

How will you be committed to developing yourself for the next 365 days/52 weeks?

Week 4 Take Action Game Plan Journal Entry

Write down three (3) commitments you will make this week to take this journey to the next level:

Commitment 1:

Commitment 2:

Commitment 3:

Daily Log

I want to challenge you with your Daily Log this week. My hopes are that you will continue this through the remainder of this book. You have options here. I would like for you to begin reading a personal development book OR watch personal development videos online. I would like you to read or watch one (1) per day, and write your takeaways from each one in your daily log:

Day 1:

Day 2:

Day 3:

Day 4:

Day 5:

Day 6:

Day 7: *Rest and Reflect Day (You will understand in Week 6 why! Be patient, do not read ahead.)*

WEEK 5 GAME PLAN:
Discovering Your Why

#noslackjusthustle

"Your WHY is your true reason and driving force!"

Parents: "Okay kiddos, it's time to go to bed!"
Children: "Why?"
Parents: "Because it's getting late."
Children: "But why can't we stay up just a little bit longer?"
Parents: "Because you need your rest."
Children: "Why?"
Parents: "So you can do well on your test tomorrow."
Children: "But why? Why? Why? Why?"

Does this type of conversation sound familiar? If you have kids or remember your childhood, then probably. Kids are very inquisitive and do a great job of asking the right questions, trying to understand and gain reason as to WHY they have to do something. The interesting thing is that most people get annoyed with this question and in a frustrated way say, *"Just because!"* They try to stop the child from continuing.

In reality, the child is right. The value in what they do is they keep asking WHY until they get to the point of fully understanding what they have to do. This is HUGE! In life, business, or anything for that matter, its' the word we use to really discover ourselves, *"WHY?!?"* *"WHY am I doing this?"*

In almost all of the **Personal Development** books that I have read, videos I have watched, or podcasts that are out there, this topic will be discussed at some point. It is the most important thing for you to discover to drive you towards success.

When you develop your WHY, I encourage you to take the same approach as a child. Go deep into your WHY. My hopes are you will go seven (7) levels deep. Ask yourself WHY seven (7) times. You will notice as you go it becomes more powerful, stronger, and you will be more emotionally attached. Now, when you get to this point and you no longer have to ask *'WHY'* anymore, then, YOU FOUND IT!

Question for Thought

The WHY activity: What is your WHY? When developing your WHY, I want you to ask yourself WHY seven (7) times. This will get you to your true WHY! Be 100% REAL with yourself!

Week 5 Take Action Game Plan Journal Entry

Write down three (3) ways you will focus on your WHY:

Ways of Focus 1:

Ways of Focus 2:

Ways of Focus 3:

Daily Log

Write down what you did everyday to focus on the value and importance of your WHY:

Day 1:

Day 2:

Day 3:

Day 4:

Day 5:

Day 6:

Day 7: *Rest and Reflect Day (You will understand next week why! Be patient, do not read ahead.)*

WEEK 6 GAME PLAN:
The 6/1 Rule

#noslackjusthustle

"Reflection is an important part of the journey."

It's Sunday night, 11:32 PM, and Jennifer is still up working on her report her boss needs on her desk by 9:00 AM Monday morning. This is the third week in a row that Jennifer has been up late the night before the report is due.

Jennifer had planned on finishing the report Friday night, but went out to dinner instead and then watched a movie. On Saturday, she went shopping with some friends all day. Now, it's crunch time, and she just got started writing the report.

Another week, another Sunday all-nighter. This has been a continuous trend for her since she started having to turn in reports on Monday's three weeks ago. Jennifer thinks to herself, maybe next week, I can get on track...

Jennifer's story is similar to some situations we all face where we work on things last minute and never have time to reflect. It's called procrastination. I have been a huge culprit of this. When we look at Jennifer's story, one thing she is missing is taking the time to rest and reflect to develop a better way of getting her report done.

Having a day to rest and reflect is so valuable in allowing you time to create a plan for the following week and to reflect on what did and did not work during the previous one.

If you believe in God, and have read the Bible, you learned that everything we know of was created in six days, and on the seventh day, God rested. This model set by the ultimate mentor is a perfect example of how I feel we should approach our own lives on a weekly basis.

You have seen and read in previous chapters so far how Day 7 is a Rest and Reflect Day. Well... here is your reasoning for it. I believe there is power in working hard toward your goals and getting things done. But, I also believe that you need time to rest and reflect so that you can relax your mind and plan.

That one day of rest and reflection does not mean that you are not working towards your goals. On the contrary, you are looking back at your week and reviewing what adjustments you need to make for the next week going forward to get better and work smarter towards your goals. This helps us not make the same mistake twice, as we just read Jennifer has been doing this for three weeks.

From here on out, make sure you really use Day 7 as a day to rest and reflect on your week, and begin preparing yourself for the next one!

Question for Thought

What is something you need to rest and reflect on from the first five weeks of your journey in this book?

Week 6 Take Action Game Plan Journal Entry

Write three (3) areas that you need to reflect on and reset your mind to make this week better than last week:

Reflection 1:

Reflection 2:

Reflection 3:

Daily Log

This is a week of reflection. Go back through the first five chapters of this book, each day rereading the chapter, your action steps, and daily log. Then, write down your reflection for each week for the provided day:

Day 1 (Reflection of Week 1):

Day 2 (Reflection of Week 2):

Day 3 (Reflection of Week 3):

Day 4 (Reflection of Week 4):

Day 5 (Reflection of Week 5):

Day 6 (Reflection of Week 6):

Day 7: *Rest and Reflect Day*

WEEK 7 GAME PLAN:
Win Your Morning

#noslackjusthustle

"Reverse engineer your morning routine to win your morning!"

"Hey Johnny, can I see you in my office?"

"Okay," Johnny replied.

Johnny walks into the Senior Vice President's office of the company he works for and sits down at her desk. She asks Johnny, *"Why were you late to work today?"*

A million thoughts ran through Johnny's mind, *"My dog was sick," "There was traffic," "My car wouldn't start."* But all of these excuses have been used by Johnny before. Johnny apologized to the Senior Vice President for being late again. She informed Johnny that this would be his last verbal warning and from here forward he will be written up if he is late.

Johnny thanks her for the warning and goes back to his desk to start his day wondering how he can fix the problem...

Has something like this ever happened to you? Have you ever been late? I know for me, something similar has happened before where I would get to work just on time. The rush in the morning was overwhelming trying to get out the door and get to where I needed to be on time, and I constantly felt as if I forgot something. My college football coach used to tell us, *"Early is on time... on time is late."* This is so true. The bigger question for all of us is what solution can we develop to get to where we need to be early, so that we are on time?

For me personally, I have tried multiple ways to achieve this. I set my alarm earlier, but there is a snooze button! I tried to get everything done the night before as well as get everything ready for my next day, but I would get distracted. These short term fixes worked for a short while, but then I would slowly fall back to my old ways.

That's when I decided to figure out how to win my morning! I came up with a way to reverse engineer my morning schedule. I knew when I had to leave to get to work early, but I also wanted to get everything done I needed to, and as a result I was able to determine when I needed to start my day.

I'm going to provide my example for you below of how I did it, and then we will get into building your reverse engineered schedule!

Here is my reverse engineered schedule, as instead of working forward, I worked backwards from 6:50 AM when I had to leave for work to be early, to determine when I needed to wake up:

Time	Task	Task List
6:50 AM	Drive To Work	~~Drive To Work~~
6:40 AM	Write Out Day's Task List	~~Get Ready~~
6:25 AM	15-Minute Business Work	~~Shower~~
6:15 AM	10-Minute Motivation / Breakfast	~~Devotional~~
5:55 AM	Get Dressed and Ready	~~10-Minute Motivation~~
5:45 AM	Shower	~~20-Minute Workout~~
5:25 AM	20-Minute Workout	~~15-Minute Business Work~~
5:15 AM	Devotional / Gratitude and Prayer	~~Write Out Day's Task List~~
5:00 AM	Wake-Up	~~Gratitude and Prayer~~
		~~Breakfast~~

After reverse engineering my schedule, I then flip my schedule so I can cross my tasks off as I complete them. Here is how my morning routine schedule looks:

Time	Task
5:00 AM	Wake-Up
5:15 AM	Devotional / Gratitude and Prayer
5:25 AM	20-Minute Workout
5:45 AM	Shower
5:55 AM	Get Dressed and Ready
6:15 AM	10-Minute Motivation / Breakfast
6:25 AM	15-Minute Business Work
6:40 AM	Write Out Day's Task List
6:50 AM	Drive To Work

Question for Thought

Are you ready to reverse engineer your morning to start your day off as a success?

Week 7 Take Action Game Plan Journal Entry

Write down your top three (3) tasks that you need to complete in the morning to make you feel good and accomplished:

Task 1:

Task 2:

Task 3:

Daily Log

On Day 1, create your morning routine through reverse engineering your morning similar to how I did to determine when you need to start your day. Write "COMPLETE" for Day 1 once you complete this task. On Day 2-6 use your newly devised schedule and write down how you felt using this new morning routine and if it was effective. If it was not effective, reflect on your schedule and make any needed adjustments (I have adjusted my initial routine 2-3 times before I found one that worked best for me.):

Day 1:

Day 2:

Day 3:

Day 4:

Day 5:

Day 6:

Day 7: *Rest and Reflect Day*

WEEK 8 GAME PLAN:
Overcome the Odds

#noslackjusthustle

"Odds were made for you to overcome them. The underdog CAN win!"

There were 3 seconds left in the game. The team had the ball on the 50 yard line, down by 5, a touchdown will win them the game and put them in the playoffs for the first time in more than 20 years. At the beginning of the season, they were expected to finish last. Here's their chance to change their team's history and future.

The team is huddled, the quarterback calls the play. Before they break, he says one word to his teammates, *"BELIEVE!"* They break the huddle, get to the line, the ball is snapped. The quarterback rolls right, dodges a tackle, heaves a long pass down the field. His wide receiver jumps for it, falls to the ground, and looks to the referee. Both hands raised in the air, signaling a TOUCHDOWN! The team goes crazy! Celebrating this unimaginable moment against all odds!

Wow! Pretty powerful story! Somewhat true, as we have seen this happen across the sports arena on many occasions. Why can't this happen to us though?

Guess what… it can! Maybe not as dramatic, but it can happen, the key word above… BELIEVE!

We all will be faced with difficult situations in life where we feel the world is against us. That's okay, and that's normal. We have a choice though, allow those feelings to defeat us, or allow those feelings to propel us.

Propel yourself forward! Believe that you can achieve your goals and overcome the odds. If you don't, then get up, and fight for it again.

I have had moments of success in life, sports, and business. I have also had moments of failure in life, sports, and business. Both were experienced with odds in my favor and when odds weren't. It's our mindset that is the driving force to set us up for success whether we succeed on the first try or the hundredth try.

You can succeed! When the odds are stacked against you. Face them head on! Believe in yourself. Give yourself a chance to win!

Question for Thought

Why do you want to overcome the odds against you to succeed?

Week 8 Take Action Game Plan Journal Entry

Write down your top three (3) "odds", or things that you feel are working against you in achieving your goals:

Odds 1:

Odds 2:

Odds 3:

Daily Log

Write down what you have worked on this week to start changing the odds of achieving your goals to be in your favor:

Day 1:

Day 2:

Day 3:

Day 4:

Day 5:

Day 6:

Day 7: *Rest and Reflect Day*

WEEK 9 GAME PLAN:
Eliminate Distractions

#noslackjusthustle

"Stay focused on the goal and what is important, distractions are put in place to stop you."

"Excuse me, John, you have a client on line one."
"I can't take the call right now, I have my daughter's dance recital to get to."
"They said it's urgent!"
"Let them know I will call them first thing in the morning. They will be my top priority."
"They said they will pull out of the deal if you don't get on the line now."
"Okay, alright, I'll take the call, but this is the last one, I have to get to the recital, I promised my daughter I'd be there."

After the call, John rushes to the recital to see his daughter, but the parking lot is empty, a promise broken, as the recital ended 15 minutes prior to his arrival.

Distractions are everywhere! We justify that they are important, but are they really what matters most? They come into our life on purpose. That purpose is to simply keep us from achieving our goals or to distract us from the things or people we value most in life.

They want to stop us from obtaining what we have set out to accomplish or love.

Eliminate the distractions!

Don't allow these distractions to get you off track. Don't allow them to get in your way! I am not saying go and quit your job or cancel your career. Absolutely not, you have to provide for your family. But... if we learned anything from the pandemic that disrupted our lives as I write this book, people will respect if you have a family commitment and the business deal can wait until the next day.

Understand that distractions will happen, but continue to push towards the goal and achieve greatness. Set goals to develop your vision of where you want to go and don't allow the distractions to get in your way.

Stay the path, ignore distractions, and start winning today!

Question for Thought

What is your biggest current distraction you currently have?

Week 9 Take Action Game Plan Journal Entry

Write down the top three (3) distractions in your life that are keeping you from your goals or what you care about most:

Distraction 1:

Distraction 2:

Distraction 3:

Daily Log

Write down every distraction that took you away from your goals each day. (Examples: Television, social media, web surfing, etc.):

Day 1:

Day 2:

Day 3:

Day 4:

Day 5:

Day 6:

Day 7: *Rest and Reflect Day*

WEEK 10 GAME PLAN:
Learning From Mistakes

#noslackjusthustle

"Learn from your mistakes and make greatness your decision."

Down to the final two for the grand prize. It's the last singer's turn to sing her song to impress the judges and the crowd. A chance for one million dollars and a record deal. The crowd is silent, the music begins, but the singer is in complete silence. She made a mistake and selected the wrong song to be played for her final performance and forgot the words. Quiet, sad, and shocked, she walks off the stage in disappointment...

Two years later, that same singer entered as a contestant on the same show, made it to the finals, and won! She fulfilled her dream of landing a record deal, because she learned from her mistake and was as prepared as ever for all of her performances!

Close your eyes... Take a step back... Think for a moment...

Is there anything you have been the best at, perfect at, mistake free at, where you did not train, practice, or work for it?

The answer is probably, NO!

We all make mistakes or showcase an imperfect moment at some point, just like the singer in the story above. The key is to learn from these mistakes.

The best way to learn is to see our own mistakes, or the mistakes of others, and work hard to not make them ourselves.

How do we learn from mistakes and get better? We practice, practice, practice, and work harder.

THE WEEKLY GAME PLAN

When you play a musical instrument, to get better, you practice. When you have a test, you study to learn and know the information. When you play a sport, you practice. When you prepare for a competition, you train. When you dance, you attend rehearsals.

Are you seeing the trend?

In order to be successful, to learn from and limit mistakes, to be the best, and perform at the highest level, we must train and practice. Learn from your mistakes and make greatness your decision!

Question for Thought

What mistakes have you made that you need to learn from?

Week 10 Take Action Game Plan Journal Entry

Write down the top three (3) mistakes you feel you have made that you need to learn from to grow:

Mistake 1:

Mistake 2:

Mistake 3:

Daily Log

Write down the mistakes you made each day (no matter how big or small) and what you will do to learn from them. (After you complete Day 6, scratch them all out, they are no more!):

Day 1:

Day 2:

Day 3:

Day 4:

Day 5:

Day 6:

Day 7: *Rest and Reflect Day*

WEEK 11 GAME PLAN:
Set Your Goals

#noslackjusthustle

"Make goals that drive results."

SNAP! John takes a picture of himself in the mirror.

He then pulls up a picture on his phone from 3 months ago when he set his goal to stay committed to eating healthy and working out once a day.

With the pictures side by side he looks and shows his wife. She gives him a big hug of excitement! He then puts measuring tape around his waist. He is now at a size 36, down from a size 40.

John's wife was so proud of him because he committed to his goal everyday to eat healthy and workout. Now, he has results to show for all of the hard work he did!

Goals…

Powerful ideas we create that can make or break us. They are how we start off our year. Some may call them *New Year's Resolutions*. We are filled with excitement and drive when we start working towards them, but the second it becomes tough, we start to fall off and think they are not attainable.

But did you know there are two types of goals: *"Result Driven Goals"* or *"Goals That Drive Results."* Same word concepts, but when repositioned, meaning two totally different things. Let's look at these goals you set.

Results Driven Goals are the goals you create that focus on getting something at the end of a set period of time.

For example: Your goal may be, *"I want to lose one (1) pound per week until I hit my goal weight."* Your goal is based on losing a specific amount of weight each week. You will start out by working your ass off to make that happen, but what happens when you stop losing one (1) pound per week? Here comes the downside. Once you start missing your goal, doubt starts to creep in. Most goals last up to 90 days and then they subside because the results do not happen.

So… what if you approached your goals with a different mindset? What if instead of creating *"Result Driven Goals"* you create *"Goals That Drive Results."*

Instead of hoping to lose one (1) pound per week, you decide that you are going to make healthier eating choices and begin working out more. There is no specific goal weight you HAVE to hit, but instead you have a specific goal of making better choices and working out more. You give yourself a process that can lead you to the change you wanted. This type of goal is a huge mentality win, because now you have something that is always achievable, simply by choice alone. As long as you choose healthier food options, and as long as you choose to work out, you have achieved your goal, and the results will end up following.

Do you see the difference in goals?

Results are important, absolutely, we want them to happen, but we do not want them to be short lived. We are looking for long term success! So let's make the change and start creating goals that drive results!

Question for Thought

What will you start implementing to change your goals from result driven goals to goals that drive results?

Week 11 Take Action Game Plan Journal Entry

Write down your top three (3) goals for the next 365 days. (Think in terms of GOALS THAT DRIVE RESULTS!):

Goal 1:

Goal 2:

Goal 3:

Daily Log

Write down what you achieved everyday towards one of your goals that drive results:

Day 1:

Day 2:

Day 3:

Day 4:

Day 5:

Day 6:

Day 7: *Rest and Reflect Day*

WEEK 12 GAME PLAN:
Your Body Is A Temple

#noslackjusthustle

"Your body is the most important car you will ever drive."

The door slammed open, and the doctor and two nurses came running into the emergency room as the 45-year old man had flatlined. The man had been in the emergency room two years ago due to health concerns. The doctors warned him then to change his dietary and work out habits. The man didn't listen.

His wife and two kids looked on, scared, nervous, praying, hoping. This had never happened before as the man was a former collegiate and professional athlete.

"CLEAR" yelled the doctor as they applied electric shock. The doctor did this two more times.

The monitor began to move, as the man was saved and his heart started to beat again! Blessed with one more shot at life, and one more shot to change his health habits. He opened his eyes, saw his wife and two children, and tears ran down his face.

It was at that moment that he decided to fully commit to his health and be there for his family!

Don't let a story like this become a reality in your life. Your body is a gift. Honor that gift, honor your body. Treat your body like a temple. Take pride in who you are and how special you are!

During your life you are blessed with one body. It is the only body you will ever have in your entire life. What does that mean to you?

I like to put it like this... *Your body is the most important car you will ever drive!* Think about that? You drive your body every single day. You use it every single day. It is important to your livelihood and ability to complete tasks.

Nurture your body. Nurture it with proper nutrition, physical activity, and rest. Your daily routine will take you where you want to go and your body to a healthier you. Make your health a part of that daily routine.

There is no price, no substitute for your health!

Your body is a temple. It is YOUR temple! Honor it in all that you do.

Question for Thought

What is the one thing you will do this week to start treating your body as the temple it truly is?

Week 12 Take Action Game Plan Journal Entry

Write down three (3) goals you have this week to start treating your body as a temple:

Body Temple Goal 1:

Body Temple Goal 2:

Body Temple Goal 3:

Daily Log

Write down what you did each day to treat your body as a temple:

Day 1:

Day 2:

Day 3:

Day 4:

Day 5:

Day 6:

Day 7: *Rest and Reflect Day*

WEEK 13 GAME PLAN:
Erase Fear

#noslackjusthustle

"Overcome fear with belief and confidence."

Backstage the introduction speaker sat waiting to speak in front of the crowd of 50,000 people. This was her first time speaking to a crowd so big. Her sister was there with her to support her on this BIG event!

The speaker looked at her sister and said, *"I have never spoken to a crowd this big before! What if I fall when I walk on stage? Will they laugh at me? What if I forget some of my speech? Will they know? I'm scared they won't clap when I am done."*

Her sister looked at her and said a short two word phrase, *"HAVE FAITH!"*

With that, the speaker took a deep breath, said the phrase quietly and repetitively to herself as she walked on stage *"HAVE FAITH, HAVE FAITH, HAVE FAITH"*

When her introduction speech was finished, she received a standing ovation! She walked backstage, gave her sister the biggest hug, and thanked her for relieving her of her fear, and helping her have faith in herself.

FEAR

By definition: To be afraid of.

Fear is a very powerful thing, a powerful thought that dwells in our minds. It can overtake us at any point in time and stop us from pushing towards our goals.

Fear itself has one goal in mind! That goal is to STOP success.

Our goal… our goal however is to overcome those fears to achieve success.

Fear is a form of doubt, self-doubt actually. It wants to let self-doubt take over and stop you from achieving great things. If we allow for the smallest seed of doubt to be planted into our minds, it grows very quickly. It grows into fear, which then shuts us down and pushes us away from what we want to do.

Don't let that happen!!!

ERASE your fears!

Focus on your goals and the outcomes that you want to see. Plant seeds of hope, of faith, and of confidence!

When you erase fear, doubt begins to wither away and is replaced with a seed of confidence.

Let that confidence reign inside of you and you will have some amazing achievements!

Question for Thought

What is your biggest fear that you need to erase from your life?

Week 13 Take Action Game Plan Journal Entry

Write down your top three (3) fears that have held you back from accomplishing things you dream of doing:

Fear 1:

Fear 2:

Fear 3:

Daily Log

Write down what you have done everyday to begin erasing the 3 fears you have that hold you back:

Day 1:

Day 2:

Day 3:

Day 4:

Day 5:

Day 6:

Day 7: *Rest and Reflect*

WEEK 14 GAME PLAN:
Be the Example

#noslackjusthustle

"People are always watching your every move, so be the example to others!"

The two old friends who shared three years of playing college football together sat down to lunch for the first time in ten years. One was now a teacher and business owner, the other a fast food chain store owner and manager. They spent time reminiscing about the fun times they had playing ball together.

When they finished eating, the store owner said, *"Before you go, I want to say thank you."*

The teacher/business owner responded, *"For what?"*

"When we were in college, you stayed after practice everyday to work hard, get better, and be an example to our team. Though I didn't follow your example when we played football, I remembered it. Thanks to you, I am where I am now because you made me realize what it takes to succeed."

Speechless, the teacher/business owner gave his old friend a hug and said, *"I'm proud of you."*

Oftentimes when we do things, there is one thing that we forget... PEOPLE ARE ALWAYS WATCHING! We live in a world where social media is constantly in our faces, and with that alone, we should understand how people are always watching.

When we do things, whether in front of our children, spouses, peers, colleagues, family, or people we don't even know, it is vitally important to be the example by word and deed. Our example may not directly impact someone in that moment, on that day, or anytime soon, but it can impact that person's life at some point.

I encourage you in all that you do, do so as if you are being the example. Approaching life this way will help you affect more people and yourself in a positive way than if you don't.

Question for Thought

How can you be an example to those you love or those that you work with?

Week 14 Take Action Game Plan Journal Entry

Write down the top three (3) ways you are going to be a positive example this week:

Example 1:

Example 2:

Example 3:

Daily Log

Write down what you did each day to be an example to others, and who you displayed that example to:

Day 1:

Day 2:

Day 3:

Day 4:

Day 5:

Day 6:

Day 7: *Rest and Reflect Day*

WEEK 15 GAME PLAN:
Find A Mentor

#noslackjusthustle

"Follow someone who already is where you want to be."

The woman took the stage to deliver one of her most amazing speeches about developing a positive mindset. As the crowd looked on, you could see the passion in her eyes. She was electrifying, and delivering one of the most inspiring messages people have ever heard.

Once the speaker concluded, she received a standing ovation for her speech. Then sitting down, she opened the conference up for a *"Q and A"* session.

She called on a gentleman who said, *"This was an amazing speech. I am fired up right now to go into the world and achieve my goals! How did you become a motivational speaker? What tips do you have for someone like me who wants to do it as well?"*

The speaker paused for a moment to think through her response, *"Thank you for your questions. I wouldn't be here today if it weren't for someone I met 15 years ago... my mentor. I was an introvert. Really good at writing speeches, but scared to death to deliver them. I would go on tour with my mentor. We toured together for 10 years. I watched and studied her every move, and listened to how she addressed the crowd. One day, she lost her voice, and couldn't go on stage. She didn't want to let the audience down, so told me to go on stage. I was scared to death! She muttered three words to me, "You are ready!" I went on stage, and felt more alive than ever, filled with passion speaking to the crowd. It was at that moment I realized that I could do it, and also the value of having a mentor! If I could give you any tips or advice. Find a mentor. Listen to them, watch them, and study them.*

Develop your belief through them so you can get to where you want to be!"

You see mentorship all the time, whether it be in coaching, acting, music, business, teaching, or any other type of work atmosphere. Learning from a mentor is a very powerful, effective method in achieving the goals you want and also developing the belief you need to achieve success, just like the story above.

Mentorship is how we evolve into something greater than we were before. When we learn from someone who has already been there, already done it, already accomplished the same things we want, the process becomes more achievable.

Now remember, this doesn't mean the process is easier or doesn't take work. But when you have a mentor, you see that the results you want can be obtained. What that does for you is it provides you with belief.

Belief is 75% of the battle, the other 25% is the work. When you believe something can happen, it is more likely to happen. Having a mentor who you can learn from helps instill that belief, and also helps show you the work you have to put in to get there.

Your goal this week is to find a mentor. If it's not someone you can talk to face-to-face, follow a mentor online. There are plenty of videos, podcasts, and books out there with great people who did great things who can start mentoring you through those avenues.

Question for Thought

What type of mentor are you going to look for to help you learn and achieve your goals?

Week 15 Take Action Game Plan Journal Entry

Write down the names of three (3) people you know or have heard of (can be anyone as long as you have access to learn from them, whether in person, online, or through reading) that you think would be a quality mentor for you to have:

Mentor 1:

Mentor 2:

Mentor 3:

Daily Log

Write down what you did each day to find a mentor that you want to learn from and follow to help you achieve your goals:

Day 1:

Day 2:

Day 3:

Day 4:

Day 5:

Day 6:

Day 7: *Rest and Reflect Day*

WEEK 16 GAME PLAN:
Make Things Fun

#noslackjusthustle

"The more fun you have doing something, the more motivated you will be to do it."

"Tammy and Billy, clean up your toys now!"

The kids have heard this phrase time and time again. This time they sternly said, *"No."*

Their dad looked at them in amazement as they have never been defiant before. He saw the sadness on their faces from him yelling at them to clean up. He thought to himself for a second and told the two young kids, *"I have an idea. Let's play a little game. I'm going to play your favorite song. You have until the song ends to have everything cleaned up. Do you think you can win the game?"*

Both Tammy and Billy's eyes lit up. They looked at each other,wiped their tears, shook their heads yes and replied, *"We can win this game."*

Dad put the music on and the kids started to clean up! They had everything away before the song ended. The best part was two things were accomplished: The room was clean and the kids had fun doing it.

In life, we are so focused on structure, what other people think, and being strict about getting certain things done. What happened to the fun we used to have as kids? We forget about it, and think that's not the way life is.

I disagree.

My opinion is life should be fun. When we do something, we should have fun doing it. Cleaning up may not be fun for you, just like how the kids didn't like it. But what if we started to think in ways like the dad did, and made the unfun activity, FUN!

When we enjoy something, we are more motivated to do it. If we dread something, we are less likely to do it. I encourage you, re-look at the tasks you need to get done and dread, and start finding ways to make them fun. Be creative!

Question for Thought

How can you change the activities you dread into activities you can have fun doing?

Week 16 Take Action Game Plan Journal Entry

Write down three (3) activities you think are fun and enjoy:

Fun 1:

Fun 2:

Fun 3:

Daily Log

Write down what you did each day to make an activity that you don't enjoy doing more fun:

Day 1:

Day 2:

Day 3:

Day 4:

Day 5:

Day 6:

Day 7: *Rest and Reflect Day*

WEEK 17 GAME PLAN:
Respect the Grind

#noslackjusthustle

"The process will be your best teaching guide"

With their heads down... sad and upset... the team just came in from losing the championship game. Their goal this season was to win the championship, but they fell one win short.

Tears are running down the players faces as they hug each other because this will be the last time they all play together as the seniors will be graduating.

Their head coach walks in... asks his players to sit with their heads held high. As they look on, the coach says the following to the team:

"Gentlemen... this year has been a pleasure getting to coach you. Do you remember the preseason? All the newspapers and sports editors picked you to be last. Where are you now? You were one (1) score away from winning the whole damn thing and being crowned champions.

In life, you will encounter many 'games'. You will win some, and you will lose some. Respect the grind, respect the process, respect what it took to get you there.

If you aren't satisfied with your outcome, then go back and look at the process. Determine what you could do differently to get the outcome you wanted. Then, go and do it!"

So many times we get caught up in the result, that we lose respect for the process. I remember when my team lost in the championship game in high school and the pain that we all felt.

We outperformed expectations of others, but not the expectations of ourselves.

It is a great thing to have high expectations. I love setting the bar high! But what I have learned throughout the years as a person, a player, a husband, a father, and a coach, is that the process is a beautiful thing that can teach us so much!

No matter what outcomes you have received, respect the grind, respect the process, learn from it, determine what you can do differently to get the outcome you want! Start grinding!

Question for Thought

What moments have you had in life where the grind/process helped you become better at something today?

Week 17 Take Action Game Plan Journal Entry

Write down the top three (3) ways you will respect the grind and learn from the process to push forward towards your goals:

Respect the Grind 1:

Respect the Grind 2:

Respect the Grind 3:

Daily Log

Write down what you did everyday to respect the grind and learn from the process to keep moving forward towards an outcome you want:

Day 1:

Day 2:

Day 3:

Day 4:

Day 5:

Day 6:

Day 7: *Rest and Reflect Day*

WEEK 18 GAME PLAN:
Discover Your Core Values

#noslackjusthustle

"The core values of a person will always unveil themselves."

The young child sat on the bed looking at her card hand. Gina had two cards left in her hand, one of which was the Old Maid.

Gina knew that the person who had the Old Maid in their hand at the end of the game lost.

Her aide had one card left as it was the last play of the game. Gina stuck out a card for her aide to take. Thinking the card was the Old Maid, the aide took the card expecting to lose.

To the aide's surprise the card Gina stuck up was the matching pair for the aide to win. Gina lost, keeping the Old Maid, but had a smile on her face.

The aide asked, *"Why did you keep the Old Maid? You could have won."*

Gina responded, *"I chose friendship over winning."*

Every time I retell this story, my eyes start to tear up. You may be asking yourself, why? The story above is based on a true story. At my 6 year old cousin's funeral, one of my cousin's therapists spoke at the funeral telling this story about how my cousin treated him in a game of Old Maid.

The entire congregation teared up at the amazement of a 6-year old boy, who was terminally ill with Leukemia, would in that moment, still choose friendship over winning. I learned more about life from this story, than any story I have heard before.

Core Values are what we live by. They are how we lead our life and how we present ourselves to others. In all situations, be aware of your core values. Stay true to them. Display them. Be an example by using them and portraying them in front of others.

Eventually, others will follow. When this occurs, positive change will start to take place. We can all impact each other by staying true to our core values. But first... we must discover what those values are!

Question for Thought

What are your most important core values?

Week 18 Take Action Game Plan Journal Entry

Write down your top three (3) core values that you care about the most:

Core Value 1:

Core Value 2:

Core Value 3:

Daily Log

Write down what you did each day to develop and showcase your core values (When we say showcase, this does not mean to boast, but rather showcase these values through actions):

Day 1:

Day 2:

Day 3:

Day 4:

Day 5:

Day 6:

Day 7: *Rest and Reflect Day*

WEEK 19 GAME PLAN: The Power of 5

#noslackjusthustle

"You are the result of the FIVE people you spend the most time with."

Mr. Smith, a young brand new teacher at the school, sat in the teachers lounge listening to the other teachers talking about the students and how bad they are. He started out excited to be a teacher, but being in the lounge for almost five months listening to all the complaints, he wasn't so sure this was a fit for him anymore.

Ms. Georgia, *"These kids these days. I can't stand them. They never listen. If they were my kid, eww wee, they would have something coming."*

Mr. Jacks agreed saying, *"Amen! If I would go back to school, there is no way I would teach."*

Mrs. Toms said, *"I don't get how anyone would want to be a teacher with how these kids act these days."*

When Mr. Smith went home that night and sat at the dinner table, all he did was complain about the kids in school and his teaching job. His parents were in shock at how he had changed, because when he first got hired he was excited to have the opportunity to make a difference in children's lives. Being around the negativity of others changed his opinion of his once known passion.

Truth be told: You are the result of the five people you spend the most time with! Think about these questions for a second. Who are the five people you are around the most? How do they act? What are their personality traits or characteristics?

When you answered the above questions did you also find the answers were also describing who you are? More than likely the answer is yes.

Your mind is constantly being trained, whether in a positive way or negative way. When you hang around people who complain, are negative, and are always down, you end up developing this same mentality.

On the flipside, if you surround yourself with people who are positive, successful, and driven, you end up developing a similar mindset.

Why is this? As people we like to fit in to the conversations that are being discussed. It is hard to go against the majority. My suggestion is to make your majority fit the type of person you want to be. If the people you currently surround yourself with aren't helping you become a better person, find new people to be around.

Believe me, this is tough, especially if some of the people were people you were close to. I am no longer friends with or even talk to a lot of people that I used to because they filled me with negativity and brought me down. Finally, I got to the point where I said to myself that I needed to find better people to be around, to grow and develop into who I want to become.

Be thoughtful in who you choose to spend your time with, your mindset depends on it!

Question for Thought

What type of person do you want to be or want to become?

Week 19 Take Action Game Plan Journal Entry

Write down three (3) traits or characteristics you want to develop and surround yourself with:

Trait/Characteristic 1:

Trait/Characteristic 2:

Trait/Characteristic 3:

Daily Log

Write down what you did each day to begin searching for your power five people that will help you develop into the person you want to be:

Day 1:

Day 2:

Day 3:

Day 4:

Day 5:

Day 6:

Day 7: *Rest and Reflect Day*

WEEK 20 GAME PLAN:
Kindness Wins

#noslackjusthustle

"The power of kindness is one of the most powerful things we all have the ability to use."

"You're out!" yelled the umpire.

This was the third out of the inning. As the teams exchanged between innings, the third base umpire walked over to the fenceline to get a drink. There was a young five-year old child with a glove on the other side of the fence jumping up and down hoping for his first foul ball!

The umpire greeted the child and asked him a few questions about if he played baseball, what position he played, and if he was staying for fireworks after the game.

After the child answered the questions, he asked the umpire, *"Could I please have a ball?"*

The umpire told the child he would get him one after the game was over. Three innings later, the game was complete, the child still there hoping for a ball. As the teams were shaking hands for a good game played, the umpire walked over to the fence line with two baseballs. He gave one to the child who was jumping up and down, and he also gave one to his sister.

This experience was one of the kindest gestures I have seen. My son was the child hopping and jumping up and down wanting a baseball. I was impressed with the umpire taking time to talk with my son and make the experience personable. Taking it one step further, not only did he stay true to his word and give my son a baseball, but he also gave one to my daughter.

The smiles on my kids' faces were priceless. This random act of kindness is what life is all about! We all have choices in life. We can choose to be kind and make people's days or we could choose to be rude and destroy people's days. The choice is ours to make every day.

I encourage you to make the choice of kindness! I said it before and I'll say it again: **People are always watching!**

Question for Thought

How can you display an act of kindness towards someone to make them feel good?

Week 20 Take Action Game Plan Journal Entry

Write down three (3) acts of kindness or rudeness you have received at some point in your life and how it made you feel:

Kindness/Rudeness 1:

Kindness/Rudeness 2:

Kindness/Rudeness 3:

Daily Log

Write down a random act of kindness that you will do each day to a random person to make them feel good:

Day 1:

Day 2:

Day 3:

Day 4:

Day 5:

Day 6:

Day 7: *Rest and Reflect Day*

WEEK 21 GAME PLAN:
Serve Others

#noslackjusthustle

"Focus on serving others rather than being served."

Waiting in line at the store now for about 30 minutes, the girl finally got her chance to buy the gift for her dad. She walks up to the cash register and puts the sweater on the belt. The sweater he has wanted for months.

After scanning the price tag, the cashier says, *"That will be thirty dollars."*

The girl looks through her purse, but only has a single twenty dollar bill. Tears start to run down her face as she says, *"Please sir, is there any way this will cover it? My dad really wanted this sweater as it reminds him of his dad, my grandfather, who passed away last year."*

Unfortunately, the cashier was not able to do anything to help the girl out. A woman standing behind her overheard the story, went into her purse and pulled out a ten dollar bill. She handed it to the cashier and said, *"This should cover it."*

With the biggest smile on her face, the girl thanked the woman behind her and happily went on her way home to deliver the special gift to her dad.

Have you ever heard a story like this before? Most likely. But they never get old. People helping people. People serving others! One of the greatest things we can do as human beings.

I know many people who do random acts of kindness all the time. Paying it forward when in line for coffee, donating to charitable causes anonymously, or giving their time to help people.

Serving others is a very powerful thing. But… be careful for your reasons that you serve others. Don't serve others in hope of getting something in return. Serve others because it is the right thing to do and you can make a positive impact.

The flipside of this though is the truth: When you serve others, you will receive great gifts in return. Remember the saying, *"You reap what you sow."* Take that phrase to the bank, and start implementing a servant mentality into your daily routine!

Question for Thought

What can you do today to have a servant mindset and begin serving others?

Week 21 Take Action Game Plan Journal Entry

Write down three (3) services you will perform this week to serve others:

Service 1:

Service 2:

Service 3:

Daily Log

Write down how you served others in your home, school, work, or community each day this week:

Day 1:

Day 2:

Day 3:

Day 4:

Day 5:

Day 6:

Day 7: *Rest and Reflect Day*

WEEK 22 GAME PLAN:
Take Responsibility

#noslackjusthustle

"Stop blaming others and start taking some responsibility."

Jeff looked on at his brother Chris getting yelled at by their dad.

"You are grounded from electronics for a week Chris. I can't believe you broke our lamp and didn't tell me sooner," yelled Jeff and Chris's dad.

"Dad, it wasn't my fault. It was an accident. The ball hit it and it fell over," Chris responded.

"Lie to me again Chris and you'll be grounded longer!" said dad.

There was a brief pause in the argument, then Jeff spoke up.

"Dad... please stop yelling at Chris. It was my fault... I broke the lamp. I let Chris take the blame for it, but it was me," Jeff said in a somber voice.

As the dad looked on, he took a deep breath and said, *"Chris, I am sorry. I wish you would have told me the truth. It was kind you were watching out for your brother, but he needs to take responsibility for his actions. Jeff, I am very disappointed in you that you were not honest from the get go, allowed your brother to take blame, and did not take responsibility for the accident. You will be grounded from electronics for 2 weeks for that."*

Jeff understood and accepted his punishment, thinking to himself he should have just taken responsibility from the beginning.

Responsibility, not a term to be thrown around lightly. In the world we live in, I have seen on so many occasions people constantly passing blame to others saying, *'It was his or her fault,' 'I didn't do it, it was him or her,' 'It's my company's fault I didn't receive a raise,' 'You are the reason we lost the game.'*

Passing blame is a coward's way out. If you work with a team of individuals whether that be in sports, school, business, or any type of job, take responsibility for your role. You control what you control, and what others do is on them.

If each team member does his or her job, and takes responsibility for what they are supposed to do, great things can be accomplished. Passing blame causes rifts between teammates or team members and results in very little getting accomplished.

Start changing your words and questions from ones that pass blame into ones that take responsibility. For example, instead of passing blame by saying, *'It's his fault we didn't score, he dropped the ball,"* take responsibility by saying, *'That's on me. I'll throw a better ball next time.'*

Question for Thought

In what areas of your life have you had difficulty taking responsibility for your actions or results?

Week 22 Take Action Game Plan Journal Entry

Write down the top three (3) areas in your life you need to start taking responsibility instead of blaming others:

Taking Responsibility 1:

Taking Responsibility 2:

Taking Responsibility 3:

Daily Log

Write down something that happened each day where you took responsibility for it rather than blaming others:

Day 1:

Day 2:

Day 3:

Day 4:

Day 5:

Day 6:

Day 7: *Rest and Reflect Day*

WEEK 23 GAME PLAN:
Develop A Childlike Perspective

#noslackjusthustle

"A child's eyes sees the world differently than adults, they see the heart of a person."

As the mom and dad looked on, they saw their son down by the ocean digging a hole collecting water. Other children of different gender, race, and ethnicity started to walk over to play too because it looked fun. As the playtime progressed, each child began to take on a role: One would dig a hole in the sand, two would get buckets of water, and another would look for crabs.

The parents looked on and smiled. This group of kids played together for about an hour. Laughing, having fun, working together, and displaying teamwork, enthusiasm, and excitement.

Let's take a further look at this childlike perspective from the story.

All four of the children came from different backgrounds, working together towards one common goal: Having fun!

Did the children know each other's names? No.

Did the children care about gender, race, or ethnicity? No.

Did the children care about political affiliation? No.

What did they care about then? They cared about having fun and helping each other out for a common goal.

The Bible says in summary: **Live life like a child**. This story is a perfect example of that. There was no hate towards each other, but rather a group of children coming together, working together, and achieving their team's goal! When hate is present, it stops people from achieving their goals and weakens the team!

My suggestion, stop buying into the crap being fed to you to hate each other. Take a childlike perspective, work together and lift each other up rather than breaking each other down!

Question for Thought

How can you begin to develop a childlike perspective in the way you interact with others?

Week 23 Take Action Game Plan Journal Entry

Write down the top three (3) childlike perspectives you feel you need to work on developing:

Perspective 1:

Perspective 2:

Perspective 3:

Daily Log

Write down how you will focus on developing a childlike perspective when interacting with others in life, work, or business each day:

Day 1:

Day 2:

Day 3:

Day 4:

Day 5:

Day 6:

Day 7: *Rest and Reflect Day*

WEEK 24 GAME PLAN:
Discover Clarity

#noslackjusthustle

"Find clarity, find power!"

Hannah was sitting at the table and praying that she wouldn't get called on stage. You could see the nervousness on her face. As the speaker walked around the room, he saw how nervous Hannah was. So... he called her up to the stage of course! She had to stand with the other nine attendees that were also called on. Nervously, she complied, and went on stage, standing with the others.

The speaker told all ten attendees who were called to the stage that the DJ would play music and they were to dance as if there was no tomorrow. He then stated, *"The goal is clear. You dance your ass off and the crowd sees it, you get to go off stage, if not, you have to remain on stage for Round 2."*

As the music played for one minute, the attendees danced. Once the music stopped, the speaker went through every individual on stage and had the crowd determine if they achieved the goal. Seven attendees stepped down, but Hannah was not one of them.

Round two was about to begin, and the speaker asked Hannah, *"The goal is clear to dance your ass off, so why aren't you going all out and achieving your goal?"*

Hannah responded, *"I'm scared and nervous of what people will think of me when I dance. Everyone is watching."*

Then the speaker said to her, *"Clarity is power! What is your goal? To dance your ass off! Get clear on that goal, and do not worry about what anyone else thinks. Your goal is yours alone! No one else's! Now make it happen!"*

This time, for Round 2, Hannah had to dance by herself. She danced her ass off! The crowd cheered like crazy! She found her clarity on the goal: *If I dance my ass off, I get off stage.* As Hannah walked off stage, she thanked the speaker and said, *"I feel more powerful than ever that I can go achieve my goals!*

In 2017, my wife and I attended an event in Sacramento, California called, *"Clarity is Power."* This event was one of the most life changing events that I have ever attended. In fact the story above is similar to one of the activities we had to do at the event. Many things that I implement in my own life and have shared with you in this book so far stemmed from what I learned at that event or from what great leaders have taught me over time.

Clarity is one of the most powerful things we can gain. Why? Because once we become clear on our goals or what we want to achieve in life, we can then start doing them!

Think about driving in a car first thing in the morning. If your windows are fogged up (unclear) are you able to drive effectively or see where you are going? No, you can't drive safely because you can't see. What happens once you defog the windows and can see clearly? You are able to start your drive to whatever destination you need to get to.

Our lives are like a fogged or clear car window. If we are not clear on our goals, like the foggy window, then it is not safe to drive our car because we may get off track or get lost. But if we are clear on our goals, like a clear window, we can see where we want to go and focus on how to get there.

Defog your mind and develop clarity. It will give you the power to achieve your goals.

Question for Thought

What do you need to find clarity in so you can start having more power over your life and goals?

Week 24 Take Action Game Plan Journal Entry

Write down the top three (3) areas you need to find clarity in:

Clarity 1:

Clarity 2:

Clarity 3:

Daily Log

Write down what you did each day to find and focus on clarity towards the goals you wish to achieve:

Day 1:

Day 2:

Day 3:

Day 4:

Day 5:

Day 6:

Day 7: *Rest and Reflect Day*

WEEK 25 GAME PLAN:
Celebrate Accomplishments

#noslackjusthustle

*"Every time a goal is reached, take a moment to celebrate it, then...
on to the next one."*

A look of determination came across Aubrie's face. She had been working for weeks to land her side aerial for the first time. Her gymnastics instructor looks on. She starts her approach, lifts off the floor with her legs in the air, and... she lands it!!!

For six weeks, Aubrie had been working, training, and listening to her instructor's words. Finally, she landed her side aerial! She looked over at her mom, who was jumping up and down with excitement!

Aubrie ran over and gave her a hug, and then went back and did it again. After her lesson was over, her mom treated her to ice cream to celebrate getting her side aerial for the first time. Filled with excitement, Aubrie couldn't wait for her ice cream. She and her mom enjoyed the time together and afterwards her mom said, *"Now it's time to get your back handspring!"*

Accomplishments feel amazing! No matter how big or how small, they deserve to be celebrated. Celebration has a positive emotional attachment to it that pushes us to want to celebrate again. Think about the first time you hit a ball, made a basket, got your first social media like on a video. All of these things deserve to be celebrated.

As parents we love to celebrate accomplishments, like when our child rolls over for the first time, starts crawling, or takes that first step. When our child does these things, we are overjoyed with excitement for them. In turn, that motivates them to do it again.

This type of excitement we have for our kids, is the same type of excitement we should have in every moment that we accomplish something! Why? Because it feels good, and it motivates a person to continue the journey and take the next step!

Question for Thought

What accomplishments have you had recently that you deserve to celebrate?

Week 25 Take Action Game Plan Journal Entry

Write down the top three (3) accomplishments you have had recently that you deserve to celebrate:

Accomplishment 1:

Accomplishment 2:

Accomplishment 3:

Daily Log

Write down an accomplishment you achieved each day, big or small, and what you did to celebrate it:

Day 1:

Day 2:

Day 3:

Day 4:

Day 5:

Day 6:

Day 7: *Rest and Reflect Day*

WEEK 26 GAME PLAN:
Stay Hungry

#noslackjusthustle

"Stay hungry, because all of the pain and hard work is worth the payoff."

The whistle blew for the last wind sprint. Each player on the team was running hard and finished all the way through.

Coach called the team in to finish practice off. He gave them a motivational speech to prepare their minds for tomorrow's game. After the team broke it down, they went inside to the locker room to go to the team dinner... except one.

One athlete stayed outside and caught 100 extra balls from the football machine. He wanted to be the best with no stone unturned. This athlete was hungry, which is why he earned the opportunity to try out professionally.

Determined, focused, driven, all synonymous with staying hungry. The moment you lose that hunger, is the moment you will begin to fall off and lose. Staying hungry, staying passionate, pushing forward towards your goal, that is how you see success.

Eating just one meal a day does not keep us filled, but eating multiple times a day does. When you have a goal you are working towards, practicing or preparing for it once does not gain achievement. To achieve this goal, you have to be hungry, day in and day out. You have to be able to push through the pain and struggle knowing that the result will be the ultimate fulfillment.

Never lose sight of your goals. Stay hungry for them, because the feeling you will get once you achieve those goals will be worth all the pain and suffering you went through to get there.

Question for Thought

What goal are you most hungry to achieve?

Week 26 Take Action Game Plan Journal Entry

Write down the top three (3) activities you have to do, to push forward, and stay hungry for your goal:

Activity 1:

Activity 2:

Activity 3:

Daily Log

Write down what you did each day this week to keep your hunger and work towards your goal:

Day 1:

Day 2:

Day 3:

Day 4:

Day 5:

Day 6:

Day 7: *Rest and Reflect Day*

WEEK 27 GAME PLAN:
Unleash the Lion Within

#noslackjusthustle

"We all have a lion inside of us, but it is those that are able to unleash it that win!"

Day after day, week after week, month after month, Matt viewed his social media pages and saw countless people succeeding in launching a business they were passionate about. But Matt was an introvert, and was nervous about putting his passion and goals onto social media for fear that he would be made fun of or that people would say negative things about him.

As time rolled on, Matt continued to just watch as others kept moving forward. Then one day he saw a post of a Lion. The Lion was roaring and had a quote reading, *"Be the king of the jungle! Unleash the Lion Within!"*

Matt leaned back in his desk chair and thought to himself, *"I can't keep waiting and watching, it's my time to unleash my lion within."* At that point, Matt made the decision to be bold, be loud, and let his passion be known as he launched his business.

Day after day, week after week, month after month, Matt was gaining more followers, getting clients, and receiving a lot of positive feedback. By unleashing the lion within, Matt far surpassed his goals and is now successfully living his dream with his biggest passion!

We all have a lion within us. Something we are passionate about or want to achieve. But many times, rather than face life like a lion, we face life like a sheep. We stay with the flock, doing what we do, sticking with the norm, and passively moving along.

Stop being a part of the norm! Start being a lion! Believe in yourself, unleash your passion within and showcase it to the world! You have greatness within you! It's time to stop hiding it and start showcasing it!

Your talents, your passions, your desires, they are inside of you for a reason... to be let out and unleashed into the world to impact lives. Now is the time to unleash... now is the time to unleash the lion within!

Question for Thought

How will you unleash the lion you have within you and start making your dreams become reality?

Week 27 Take Action Game Plan Journal Entry

Write down the top three (3) things you need to do to be able to unleash the lion within:

Unleash the Lion 1:

Unleash the Lion 2:

Unleash the Lion 3:

Daily Log

Write down what you did every day to help you prepare to unleash the lion you have within you:

Day 1:

Day 2:

Day 3:

Day 4:

Day 5:

Day 6:

Day 7: *Rest and Reflect Day*

WEEK 28 GAME PLAN:
Embrace Trials

#noslackjusthustle

"Embrace your trials, they have a purpose!"

As the applicant walked out the door, her head was down, with tears flowing from her eyes down her cheeks. Another interview to be a teacher, another let down. She had substitute taught at the school for the past six months and thought that this would be her opportunity.

Upset, she entered her car thinking to herself that this was the fifth interview and no job yet. Her students loved her, parents and administrators complimented her, but she was unable to land a job.

Two years later... She received a full time teaching job. During that two year time frame she continued to substitute teach and worked with children who had special needs. Now, she has a job teaching special needs children in a very reputable school district.

In that two year time frame, the former school she substitute taught at and did not get hired at actually shut down for testing fraud and violations. She didn't realize it then, but what she learned as a substitute teacher and working with special needs kids during that time, where she was facing this trial, prepared her for her future success!

Understand that trials are not the end of the story. They are part of the journey while the story is still being written.

Everyone faces trials at some point in their life. These trials help to develop our character, they make us stronger, and they allow us an opportunity to grow and be able to help others who may face similar trials as well as discover a passion we may not have been aware of yet.

Embrace your trials!

Remember, every trial has a purpose!

Question for Thought

How will you embrace the trials you are facing and work to overcome them?

Week 28 Take Action Game Plan Journal Entry

Write down the top three (3) "trials" that you are currently going through and need to overcome:

Trial 1:

Trial 2:

Trial 3:

Daily Log

Write down what you have worked on this week to start overcoming the trials you are facing:

Day 1:

Day 2:

Day 3:

Day 4:

Day 5:

Day 6:

Day 7: *Rest and Reflect Day*

WEEK 29 GAME PLAN:
Remain Humble

#noslackjusthustle

"The greater the success, the more humble you should remain."

The crowd roars as the referee's hands go up signaling another touchdown! This was Aiden's fourth touchdown of the game putting his team up 27-0 going into the fourth quarter. Last week he was the city's player of the week with a three touchdown performance.

The clock reads 0:00, the whistle blows, and the game ends. After the game is over, the fans rush the field as the team is now conference champions! Aiden's best friend finds him and says, *"Man, if it wasn't for you, this team would be nowhere."*

Aiden responds, *"No way man. Without the line or my teammates, I would never score. They are the reason I have had a great year!"*

When we see success it is very hard sometimes to remain humble. We feel good and we get overwhelmed with joy. The key is to remain humble in these situations. At any moment, at any time, our success can go away.

As a coach, I always said this to my athletes, ***"Take the responsibility, pass the praise."***

What did I mean? If something goes wrong, take responsibility for it, whether it was your fault or not. If something goes right, pass the praise along. During my senior year of high school, our football team was very successful, and I had the honor of being the team's quarterback.

Week in and week out, if we ever did not play well, or made a mistake, I would take full responsibility for it. My teammates will tell you. If a player dropped a pass, I would put it on me that it was a bad throw.

When we performed well, I would always pass the praise. If I was interviewed by the news and they asked me about how good I played, I would always pass the praise to my teammates.

Why?

I understood the value of remaining humble and realized that my successes were not only a result of my efforts, but a result of our entire team putting forth the effort.

So, next time you see success, remember to stay humble and appreciate it! This attribute will lead you to see even more success!

Question for Thought

In what areas or life, work, or sports have you seen success and need to remain humble in?

Week 29 Take Action Game Plan Journal Entry

Write down the top three (3) areas or successes you need to humble yourself in:

Area/Success 1:

Area/Success 2:

Area/Success 3:

Daily Log

Write down how you will display humility each day when you achieve a goal or success:

Day 1:

Day 2:

Day 3:

Day 4:

Day 5:

Day 6:

Day 7: *Rest and Reflect Day*

WEEK 30 GAME PLAN:
Release Your Worries

#noslackjusthustle

"The day you stop worrying will be the day you start living!"

What a beautiful sound it was! The crowd stood up once the musical performer was done playing to give him a standing ovation! The musician was only in eighth grade, but was receiving recognition and awards for how well he played his instrument.

A month later, back at school, getting ready to select classes for the upcoming year, the same musician chose not to take band class anymore. The musician was also a star athlete on the football and basketball teams. His teammates constantly made fun of him for playing an instrument.

The musician/star athlete chose, instead of participating in both, to only play sports because he was worried that he would get made fun of by his friends. What his friends didn't know was that his true passion was music, not sports. He would never touch an instrument again.

A dream, a future, altered by the worry of what others think. Looking back at that story, I would bet that those friends who made fun of him are most likely not friends with him anymore anyway. So he gave up his passion for people who are no longer in his life.

I understand… you may be thinking that we cannot predict if we will still be friends or not friends with people when we are in the moment. I agree with this. But here is my counter. No matter your family, friends, or whomever is in your life, there are ONLY two (2) people that will be with you every single second, of every single minute, of every single day. Those people are you and God. Therefore, I believe that these are the only two people you should ever worry about pleasing!

Now let's get to the truth about releasing your worries. Once your worries are gone, lifted from you, the weight is off of your chest... you can breathe again and experience life to its fullest. You start making decisions based on your happiness rather than what others will think of you.

Too many times we get caught up in worrying about what other people think of us. This is a waste of time and a waste of value. We ask questions like: *Will they make fun of me? Are they going to like my hair? Do they think my dress is pretty?*

Stop asking the questions about what others will think of you, and start asking the questions about what you think of you: *Am I happy? Do I like how my hair looks? Is this dress something I want to wear?*

Release your worries *(truly, don't just say you will, actually do it)* and watch the amazing change you will experience!

Question for Thought

What worries do others have over you that you need to release?

Week 30 Take Action Game Plan Journal Entry

Write down the top three (3) worries you have in regards to what other people think about you or what you do:

Worry 1:

Worry 2:

Worry 3:

Daily Log

Write down what you did each day to release your worries about what others think of you:

Day 1:

Day 2:

Day 3:

Day 4:

Day 5:

Day 6:

Day 7: *Rest and Reflect Day*

WEEK 31 GAME PLAN:
Stay Consistent

#noslackjusthustle

"Consistency will keep you in rhythm."

THUMP! Baby Lisa fell right on her butt as her parents looked on and smiled. She puts her hands on the couch, pushes herself up and... THUMP! On her butt again. This is the fifth time in a row she fell on her butt.

Again, Baby Lisa pushes her way up... is a little wobbly... and then... puts her right foot in front of her left foot, then her left foot in front of her right foot! After that she falls, but her parents jump up with joy and give her a great big hug and kiss!

This was Baby Lisa's very first step! She had been trying it for one week now, and finally, she did it! Her parents were so excited and proud of her!

As a parent this is one of the most precious moments when we see our child take his or her first step! It begins a new journey of exploration. But, how does the child even get there? By being consistent.

When a child falls on their butt, they don't quit trying to walk. Instead they get up and try it again. They consistently keep trying until they achieve their goal of taking that first step.

A child is born with determination and consistency. They are determined to achieve something (sitting up, crawling, walking, etc.), and they are also consistent in attempting to do it.

This childlike consistency is valuable for us adults to pay attention too. We often forget that it doesn't always take just one time to achieve something. It takes consistency, continuous effort to reach that goal.

When we approach life or our goals, it is valuable to stay consistent and continue to work towards them, because we are only just a child's step away!

Question for Thought

What areas in your life right now do you have trouble being consistent in?

Week 31 Take Action Game Plan Journal Entry

Write down the top three (3) areas in your life where you need to be more consistent to help you in achieving your goals:

Consistency 1:

Consistency 2:

Consistency 3:

Daily Log

Write down what you did each day to be consistent with working towards your goals and things you want to achieve:

Day 1:

Day 2:

Day 3:

Day 4:

Day 5:

Day 6:

Day 7: *Rest and Reflect Day*

WEEK 32 GAME PLAN:
Do It Right

#noslackjusthustle

"Make excellence an everyday habit, not an occasional act."

The little boy walked to the pitcher's mound to get ready to practice fielding. His dad yelled over to him, *"Come here son."*

He ran over to his dad and responded, *"Yeah dad?"*

His dad said, *"Son... in everything you do, do it right. Make excellence an everyday habit. I don't care how anyone else acts on this field. You be the example, you set the tone. I watched you walk out to the pitcher's mound. You never walk. You run as fast as you can out there. You be excellent in everything you do and try. You may not always win, but you will never question your effort. Now go back out there son. Do it right. Be excellent and run as fast as you can to that pitcher's mound."*

The little boy ran as fast as he could to the pitcher's mound as his dad looked on with a smile.

We have all heard the phrase, *"Stop going through the motions."* But how many times do we see others *"just going through the motions"* and get caught doing it ourselves? If you need to, go back to Week 19 and reread, *"The Power of 5"* to stop getting caught in this trap of following the wrong people.

There is a simple rule to live by and act by: DO IT RIGHT! When you do something, do it right. Don't half ass it, don't be lazy, you do it right.

Expect excellence and greatness from yourself. That starts by doing things right. If you consistently are doing something half ass, you will grow to always do it half ass. Do things right.

Develop higher expectations for yourself. It's easy to be average and forgotten. The most successful people though are the ones that don't quit, work hard, and focus on doing things right!

Question for Thought

What things have you been doing lazy and need to start doing right?

Week 32 Take Action Game Plan Journal Entry

Write down the top three (3) things you need to start doing right:

Do It Right 1:

Do It Right 2:

Do It Right 3:

Daily Log

Write down what you did each day to start doing things the right way:

Day 1:

Day 2:

Day 3:

Day 4:

Day 5:

Day 6:

Day 7: *Rest and Reflect Day*

WEEK 33 GAME PLAN:
Replace Excuses with Reasons

#noslackjusthustle

"Excuses are weakening, while reasons are strengthening."

"I can't workout today, I don't have enough time" - Excuse
"I only have 10 minutes, so I am going to do a quick workout to stay in shape." - Reason

"I can't right now, I'll get to that tomorrow." - Excuse
"That's important to you. I'll be done in 5 minutes, then I'll get that done for you." - Reason

"It's okay if I miss a day, it's not that big of a deal, no one will know." - Excuse
"I committed to doing this everyday. I will know if I did or didn't do it." - Reason

"I knew I would get a D, I didn't really try." - Excuse
"I earned the grade based on my effort. Next time, I will try even harder to do better." - Reason

Excuses versus reasons... How many times have we made the excuse statement? We all have done it. You have, I have, we all have at some point. But how simple is it to change that excuse to not do something into a reason to do something?

Find a reason! Replace every excuse you have not to do something, with a reason to do something. This will make you stronger, more dedicated, and more focused on achieving your goals.

Oftentimes we fear our goals, and put them off with excuses, because we think to ourselves, *"What if I don't achieve my goal."* The better question is, *"What happens when I achieve my goal?!?"*

We are more than halfway through our journey. Start replacing your excuses with reasons if you haven't done so already!

Question for Thought

What excuses do you find yourself making that are stopping you from achieving your goals?

Week 33 Take Action Game Plan Journal Entry

Write down the top three (3) excuses you currently make, and then three (3) reasons you will replace those excuses with:

Excuses / Reason 1:

Excuses / Reason 2:

Excuses / Reason 3:

Daily Log

Write down a reason statement you made each day to have a reason to do something or work towards your goal:

Day 1:

Day 2:

Day 3:

Day 4:

Day 5:

Day 6:

Day 7: *Rest and Reflect Day*

WEEK 34 GAME PLAN:
Keep Life Fresh

#noslackjusthustle

"The more you enjoy yourself, the more you enjoy life, the more you enjoy others."

The car pulls into the airport. The husband opens the door and takes the blindfold off from covering his wife's eyes. She looks on in confusion and asks, *"Why are we at the airport?"*

"We are going on a date this weekend," the husband replies.

"Oh my gosh! Where?" asked the wife.

"We are flying to Miami beach for the weekend to get away and enjoy each other!"

The wife gives her husband a big hug and kiss as they get ready to enter the airport for their trip. She was shocked, excited, and filled with emotion because they are going on a trip to her surprise, and she had no idea about it!

What a great story on how to keep life fresh. Now… taking a big time trip down to Miami doesn't have to be the only way to keep life fresh, but it emphasizes the point.

Earlier we talked about the value of a routine (Refer to Week 7: Win Your Morning). Which I am definitely a proponent of, but… being spontaneous is pretty cool too! It doesn't have to be taking a big trip or something super expensive. But it is exciting to go against the norm of the consistent routine and do something new, fresh, and exciting.

I've said it before, and I'll say it again. Life is about creating moments. Moments are what will always carry on with you! So keep life fresh by ditching the routine (on some occasions, not everyday now) and do something new, fun, and exciting. You, your spouse, your family, they will thank you for it!

Question for Thought

What can you do on a monthly basis to keep life fresh for yourself, you and your spouse, your family, or even your business?

Week 34 Take Action Game Plan Journal Entry

Write down the top three (3) spontaneous ideas you have that are fun and will keep life fresh:

Spontaneous Idea 1:

Spontaneous Idea 2:

Spontaneous Idea 3:

Daily Log

You have worked so hard this far! This is your week to take a moment and keep life fresh for yourself, you and your spouse, or your family! Write down how you will keep life fresh each day this week, then commit to keeping life fresh one (1) random day per month, from here on out!

Day 1:

Day 2:

Day 3:

Day 4:

Day 5:

Day 6:

Day 7: *Rest and Reflect Day*

WEEK 35 GAME PLAN:
Make a Great Day

#noslackjusthustle

"Don't have a great day, make a great day!" - Coach Christopher Smith

Jessica jumped out of bed, excited for her day. Everything was planned out, she was going to take a walk at the park, meet her mom for lunch, go to the gym, and then go out to dinner with friends.

She completed her morning routine, got ready to go, opened the front door to head to the park and it started to rain heavily. Her entire day was set until this happened, and her walk at the park was going to set the tone for a great day. But now she can't walk due to the weather. Jessica was frustrated and bothered as her entire day and plan of events had changed.

Taking a deep breath, she paused for a minute, and thought to herself, *"How can I make the best of this situation?"*

After taking a few minutes to ponder this question, she decided she was going to drive to the local mall to get her walk in and buy her a new outfit for this evening's dinner outing with her friends.

The situation was not ideal, but Jessica chose to make the best of the situation, and created an awesome day!

You have the choice everyday to decide how your day is going to go. Think about the phrase my college head football coach would always tell us as players, *"Don't have a great day, make a great day!"*

At the time of hearing this in college, my teammates and I used to chuckle and rub this phrase off thinking, *"What is coach talking about?"* Now, looking back, it makes perfect sense, and I'm glad I am able to understand what he meant!

Everyday we wake up and have a choice. The choice is simple: We can make the day great or not. Our day is under our control. Are there outside forces that can affect our day? Potentially. But we have full control over how we respond to those forces that may affect us.

There is a definitive difference between having a great day or making a great day. Having a great day is whatever comes your way will affect your day and hopefully all will go well for you. Making a great day gives you full control over your day, your attitude towards it, and what you will accomplish no matter what the circumstances.

So again, in the words of my college coach, *"Don't have a great day, make a great day!"*

Question for Thought

What are you going to do today to make it a great day?

Week 35 Take Action Game Plan Journal Entry

Write down the top three (3) ways you can take control of your day to make it a great day:

Great Day Control 1:

Great Day Control 2:

Great Day Control 3:

Daily Log

Write down what you did each day to make it a great day:

Day 1:

Day 2:

Day 3:

Day 4:

Day 5:

Day 6:

Day 7: *Rest and Reflect Day*

WEEK 36 GAME PLAN:
One Week to Live

#noslackjusthustle

"Live in every moment as if it is the last moment."

John opened the front door, walked into his house, dropped his briefcase, and gave his wife the biggest hug possible. Moments earlier, John found out that he had a terminal illness, and doctor's were unsure how long he would live for. They used the term, *"Weeks.'*

His wife said to him, *"Let's live and enjoy every last moment we have together."*

John replied, *"Let's do it. We can't look back, but I wish we had thought this way our entire marriage."*

From then on, John and his wife lived everyday as if it was their last together. Five years have passed, and John is still staying strong. A terminal illness thought to take his life weeks later, he is still pushing forward, living every moment with his family as if it is his last. Because... one day it will be, but not yet.

How many times do we look back and WISH for more time? Don't get caught up in this mindset and miss the moments you can create.

Life is a series of moments. They will create happiness or sadness, excitement or boredom, memories or emptiness, and it is on us as to what is created.

We are not guaranteed the next second, let alone the next day or week. But yet, we get caught up putting off the things we love, the people we care about, or the dreams we have. Why? Because we think tomorrow will come and is guaranteed to us. If we learned anything at the start of the 2020's, we learned nothing is guaranteed!

Think of the enjoyment and moments you can create if you lived every day or week as if you only had one week left to live. What would you accomplish? What memories would you create with your family? When I say this, I'm not saying to blow all of your money away. You can create many memories without doing that. I'm saying, approach every day as if you had one week to live, see what you get done, and what new memories you create!

Question for Thought

If you only had one (1) week to live, what would you do?

Week 36 Take Action Game Plan Journal Entry

Write down the top three (3) moments you would want to create in your life if you only had one week left to live:

Moment 1:

Moment 2:

Moment 3:

Daily Log

Write down what you did each day to live as if you only had one week left to live:

Day 1:

Day 2:

Day 3:

Day 4:

Day 5:

Day 6:

Day 7: *Rest and Reflect Day*

WEEK 37 GAME PLAN:
Be Energetic

#noslackjusthustle

"People will feed off of your energy, whether positive or negative."

"For thine is the kingdom, the power, and glory forever, Amen!"
The team finishes team prayer prior to the Head Coach's
pregame speech. All players are on one knee, looking up to their
coach anticipating his words for the Homecoming Football
Game.

The coach looks at each of his players and begins...

*"Homecoming... Tonight's the night... Tonight's the night
gentlemen when the ghosts of the past will rise up! They rise up to
see you! All the tradition, all the pain, all the glory, it's all a part of
tonight and the game you are about to embark on...*

{The coach's voice begins to grow louder}

*There is nothing better than to go out in front of your home
crowd, your alumni, your classmates, your community on
Homecoming, and bring home a victory!*

{The coach's voice grows even louder}

*The other team is going to try to take that away from you. DON'T
LET THEM! You have worked too hard for this moment!*

*When the game is over... when that scoreboard hits zero... when
the ghosts of the past return to their home... when the fans are on
their way out... make sure you have left EVERYTHING on that
field!*

Because tonight is your night and everyone is here for you! LET'S GOOOOOOOOO!!!!"

{The team screams at the top of their lungs and storms out to take the field}

WOOOOOO! I love a GREAT pregame speech!

I will never forget when I was a Junior in college. We are getting ready for our Saturday afternoon football game. Our team just came in from our pre-game warm-up. We are sitting in the team meeting room and our coach comes in to deliver his pre-game speech.

As he talked, his energy continued to build. Then... out of nowhere, he pulls out a huge club that looks like BamBam's from The Flintstones, and BOOM! He breaks one of the tables with the club.

It was totally awesome! Our entire team was taken back for a moment because we never saw this intensity from the coach before. There was a brief second pause once he hit the table where we all looked at each other confused. Then we just all started to scream and go wild with excitement! We were so energized for the kickoff of that game, we went out and brought home a victory. I'll never forget the club! Haha!

The power of energy and emotion are crucial to success. Not all energy is good though. Negative energy will give off the wrong vibe and detract people from wanting to be around you. Positive energy though, positive energy can attract the people you want to be around and make the difference in people wanting to work with you or not. BE ENERGETIC!!!

Question for Thought

How can you display positive energy to others to start getting people excited?

Week 37 Take Action Game Plan Journal Entry

Write down the top three (3) ways you can showcase high energy to others in a positive way:

Be Energetic 1:

Be Energetic 2:

Be Energetic 3:

Daily Log

Write down what you did each day to be energetic and display positive energy:

Day 1:

Day 2:

Day 3:

Day 4:

Day 5:

Day 6:

Day 7: *Rest and Reflect Day*

WEEK 38 GAME PLAN:
Law of Attraction

#noslackjusthustle

"How you act, is what you attract!"

Jeff had just finished his first personal development book. He was excited, pumped, and filled with energy!

He got in his car to drive to his client's house. Jeff put on some inspirational and positive music to bump to as he was driving. What Jeff didn't realize as he was singing the current song was that he was going about ten miles per hour over the speed limit.

Lights display in his rear view mirror and Jeff pulls over immediately realizing he was going too fast. Instantly, Jeff gets his information out for the officer and prays to God, *"God, I love the positivity that you are giving me right now! Let's make today great! I'm excited for today."*

Understanding that he was in the wrong, he understood that he would probably get a fine and/or ticket. The officer approached the car, and kindly asked for Jeff's information. Jeff apologized to the officer and told him how he totally missed the speed limit change from 45mph to 35 mph (which was true).

The officer performed his duties running a plate check and all. Then he walked back to Jeff's car and said, *"Jeff, you have a clean driving record. So I'm going to let you off with a warning here, but please watch your speed."*

Jeff humbly thanked the officer and wished him a great rest of the day. As Jeff drove off he understood more than ever the Law of Attraction!

The Law of Attraction... you have probably heard about it or read about it in almost every personal development book, podcast, or video that you have read or viewed. The story above was an actual account of an event that happened to me.

So based on my personal experiences, believe me when I say: **The Law of Attraction is true!** Think about all the things that have happened to you in the past week, month, or even year. Some have been positive, some negative. The truth is, whatever it was, it was attracted to you in some way.

How many times have you heard someone say, *"I screwed up again,"* or *"Why do bad things always happen to me?"*

The reason these things happen is because the individual is so focused on them, that no matter what, it's inevitable that something is going to happen within that realm of thought.

As the old saying goes, *"Think before you act."* Why don't we change that phrase to, *"Think and you will attract!"*

Question for Thought

How can you start reshaping your mind using the Law of Attraction to start attracting what you want, rather than what you don't want?

Week 38 Take Action Game Plan Journal Entry

Write down the top three (3) ways you can change your thinking to start implementing the Law of Attraction and start attracting what you want:

Law of Attraction Thought 1:

Law of Attraction Thought 2:

Law of Attraction Thought 3:

Daily Log

Write down what you did each day to use the Law of Attraction to start attracting what you want:

Day 1:

Day 2:

Day 3:

Day 4:

Day 5:

Day 6:

Day 7: *Rest and Reflect Day*

WEEK 39 GAME PLAN:
The Creed for Success

#noslackjusthustle

"A CHAMPION is built from hard work and dedication!"

The Creed for Success by Jon Zeal

In order for me to succeed, I need to grow.
In order for me to grow, I need to change.
In order for me to change, I need to take action.
In order for me to take action, I need to identify what needs changed.
In order for me to identify what needs change, I need to be willing.
In order to be willing, I need to humble myself.
In order to humble myself, I need to see the problem.
In order to see the problem, I need to have realization.
So, in order for me to succeed, I need to realize I have a problem, humble myself, and be willing to identify what I need to change and take the action to change. Then I will grow. Then I will have success!

BOOM! Wow! Those are some powerful words from my friend Jonathan Sickmeyer, who shared this with me and some other friends on a LIVE video. HUGE shout out to Jon for allowing me to share this with all of you.

As we continue to come closer to the end of this journey, I thought this was the perfect place to share with you this amazing creed for success!

I encourage you to read this creed through and through at least seven times (a minimum of one time per day). Hopefully, you will read it twice per day: First thing in the morning when you get up, and last thing at night before going to bed.

Implement *The Creed for Success*, continuing growing from now through the end of this book, and be excited with all that happens!

Question for Thought

What emotions and thoughts ran through your mind as you read The Creed for Success?

Week 39 Take Action Game Plan Journal Entry

Write down the top three (3) things you need to identify within yourself to change and start growing:

Growth Identification 1:

Growth Identification 2:

Growth Identification 3:

Daily Log

Write down what you felt each day when you read The Creed for Success again:

Day 1:

Day 2:

Day 3:

Day 4:

Day 5:

Day 6:

Day 7: *Rest and Reflect Day*

WEEK 40 GAME PLAN:
The Standard

#noslackjusthustle

"Do not sacrifice your standards, your standard is your standard!"

Bill Thompson, the star quarterback of his high school football team, walked into the Head Coach's office before practice and sat in the chair in front of the coach's desk.

"Do you know why I called you in here today Bill?" said the Head Coach.

"I'm not sure sir, but I have an idea," replied Bill as he looked glum in expectation waiting for what his coach would say.

"We have a standard here at Prep High for all of our athletes. At the beginning of this season, you signed a contract with those standards. Yesterday, you violated one of them by skipping school for Senior Skip Day. Our players look up to you as a leader. You chose to skip school and practice to celebrate Senior Skip Day rather than be here with your team. As a leader of this team, following the standards, and holding yourself at a high standard is huge for your time here, and even more so when you enter adult life. Based on our team rules, you will not play in the first half of the game due to your violation of the standards," stated the coach.

"But I'm sorry coach, I didn't think it was that big a deal. I mean, I'm a senior. Can't I just sit out the first series?"

The head coach replied, *"No Bill. If I let that happen, then me as a leader of this team would have not kept the standard we have created. It would be unfair to others who have received the same discipline for the same behavior, and it allows other athletes to think this is okay."*

"Alright coach, I understand. That second half, I will dominate and make it up to you," replied Bill.

Prep High was down by two touchdowns at half, but Bill came in the second half and helped lead his team to victory. He went on to play college ball and was a team captain creating his team's slogan, *"KEEP THE STANDARD!"*

This is one of my favorite topics to discuss with people, **The Standard.** Too many times I have seen people fail because they decide to adjust their standards or lower their standards. As a result, things change, usually for the worse, and what they previously built falls apart.

Keep your standards! You have them for a reason, stick to them. If you are a coach, and your standard is that if an athlete gets written up at school they miss a quarter or inning of play, then stick to that standard! Once you let the standard go, you open the door for other athletes to make the same mistakes and get away with them because they have the leverage to say that you let it go before. So stick to your standards!

The same mindset applies if you are a business owner and have certain standards of expectations for the vendors you use, stick to them!

Do not sacrifice your standards! And NEVER sacrifice your standards for a quick dollar either, you will lose more in the long run than the short gain you receive. Keep your standards the way you want them, and always remain true to that level of expectation!

Question for Thought

Whether you are a coach, a business owner, or whatever position you may hold, what is your expected standard within that realm?

Week 40 Take Action Game Plan Journal Entry

Write down the top three (3) standard expectations you have within the realm you work or do business in:

Standard 1:

Standard 2:

Standard 3:

Daily Log

Write down what you did each day to stay true to the standard expectations of yourself or others within your realm of work or business:

Day 1:

Day 2:

Day 3:

Day 4:

Day 5:

Day 6:

Day 7: *Rest and Reflect Day*

WEEK 41 GAME PLAN:
Find A Tribe

#noslackjusthustle

"Find a tribe of like minded people to help push you towards success!"

Brooke rushed into the house, ran upstairs to her office, and got to her computer quickly. She had just come home from her full time job, but was even more excited to get on her meeting with a group she had recently joined called: *Female Entrepreneurs Now and for the Future.*

This was her first call with them! She had her professional attire on as she wanted to impress everyone because she would be introducing herself to the group for the first time.

The call started, and there were ten other entrepreneurs on the call. They all shared their story, their goals, their passions, and what they are striving to accomplish.

Finally, it got to Brooke. She introduced herself and shared all of her information. The group was very supportive of her, and one lady on the call even personally messaged Brooke to set up a time to speak afterwards about mentoring her.

Brooke felt amazing! She had finally found a group of people that she could relate to and grow with! This was the beginning of a special journey for her!

Brooke's story is awesome, and more common than we think. Building a tribe or finding a tribe of like-minded people to interact with consistently is an amazing thing. It's basically a group of accountability partners that will help you stay positive, keep working towards your goals, and remain motivated, like Brooke experienced.

Do your research though, don't just join a group to join a group. You have to have a purpose and be a part of something where people share the same core values. Refer back to Week 18 where you discovered what core values you have. Use these to help you find a group of people that align with you and will be a positive impact for you.

Currently, I am part of a tribe called, *"Mike's Inner Circle."* This is a group of like-minded entrepreneurs where we share similar mindsets and core values. We meet one to two times per month to give updates on our business, provide support to each other, and discuss our next month's plan. There are also a group of millionaires that we meet with who teach us their success strategies to help us diversify what we do!

A tribe is a very powerful community to be a part of, and now that we are just weeks away from concluding this journey, start thinking about the tribe you want to create or join!

Question for Thought

What do you want to look for in a tribe of people to help make you better and reach your goals?

Week 41 Take Action Game Plan Journal Entry

Write down the top three (3) mindset related attributes you want to look for in a tribe to be a part of:

Attribute 1:

Attribute 2:

Attribute 3:

Daily Log

Write down each day one attribute or value you would like to see with the tribe you create or join, start attracting that now:

Day 1:

Day 2:

Day 3:

Day 4:

Day 5:

Day 6:

Day 7: *Rest and Reflect Day*

WEEK 42 GAME PLAN:
Little Decisions

noslackjusthustle

"The big picture is made up of little decisions."

"Today is the day I'm going to launch my first business." Tim thought to himself.

He wrote down his goals of owning a multi-million dollar business, but wasn't sure how to get there since he didn't even have a dollar. Tim decided to make a decision. For all of his adult years, he set his alarm for 6:00am to get his morning routine and day started. He decided to make a little adjustment. He would now wake up at 4:30am everyday so he can get an extra 90 minutes to work on his business.

During this 90 minutes, Tim would make many little decisions and work on many little tasks for his business he launched. As time went on, this initial little decision of adding 90 minutes to his work time resulted in big gains! After one month, he made his first hundred dollars. After one year, he made his first thousand. After two years he made over one hundred thousand dollars. Now, five years into his business, focusing on little decisions, he has made over one million dollars!

Every little decision we make paints the bigger picture of our life. I feel that's why the Bible discusses this point... *Be quick to listen, slow to speak.* I think this statement relates to making little decisions and how we should approach life. Rather than try to do things super fast or just try to get things done, switch the focus to accomplishing small tasks effectively and let the results build from there.

As people, we always want the big rewards. But the only way to truly earn those big rewards is by making and focusing on the little decisions.

You may have a goal of having a million dollar business. That's great, and I believe you should have that goal. But before you can have a million dollar business, you need a hundred thousand dollar business, a ten thousand dollar business, a thousand dollar business, a hundred dollar business, a ten dollar business, a one dollar business. Do you see the process when we work backwards?

Every little decision or little bit of progress will help paint the bigger picture. And with the dollar reference above, each time you hit one of those landmarks CELEBRATE (Refer to Week 25: Celebrate Accomplishments)!

So be sure to think through and enjoy the little decisions you make so you can have a beautiful work of art when everything is all said and done!

Question for Thought

What is your big picture you want to paint, and what little decisions can you make to help get you there?

Week 42 Take Action Game Plan Journal Entry

Write down the top three (3) little decisions that you need to make to get things started towards the bigger picture you want to paint:

Little Decision 1:

Little Decision 2:

Little Decision 3:

Daily Log

Write down the little decisions or the little tasks that you completed each day that are going to help you paint the bigger picture for your goals:

Day 1:

Day 2:

Day 3:

Day 4:

Day 5:

Day 6:

Day 7: *Rest and Reflect Day*

WEEK 43 GAME PLAN:
The Snowball Effect

#noslackjusthustle

"Momentum builds momentum!"

STRIKE! Every pin fell again. That's Anna's third strike in a row! She has really gotten into a rhythm. Her first two rolls ended in a split. But now, she is mounting a comeback.

She finished the match having bowled ten strikes in a row to help her complete an amazing comeback to win the Bowling Championship.

After receiving her trophy, the sports reporter asked Anna, *"How were you able to come back from being down to win the match?"*

Anna responded, *"I started to gain some momentum and just felt it. I couldn't stop, and I rattled off 10 straight strikes!"*

This chapter is fitting to follow up our previous week's chapter about *Little Decisions.* **The Snowball Effect** is about taking those little decisions or positive things happening in your life, and allowing the momentum to build.

You see **The Snowball Effect** in sports all the time, just like our bowling story above. As a team gets into a rhythm, and starts building momentum, they see better results. **The Snowball Effect** has sparked some of the best comebacks in sports history! And it's all due to momentum.

Think about it. A snowball starts rolling down a hill of snow. As the snowball rolls, it will collect more and more snow. It will get bigger and also pick up more speed. This is the effect momentum can have on your life. If you start experiencing and focusing on positivity, more positive things will occur for you. **The Snowball Effect** as momentum builds momentum!

As you do things or complete tasks, let the momentum build for you. Keep the snowball rolling. If you stop abruptly, everything will fall apart, just like a snowball, it will break and stop moving. So I encourage you to keep going. Keep letting the momentum build for you into bigger and greater things! **The Snowball Effect** can be very powerful for you and your goals, if you let that momentum build!

Question for Thought

What is an area or goal that you have where you want The Snowball Effect to help you build momentum?

Week 43 Take Action Game Plan Journal Entry

Write down the top three (3) areas you need momentum in to achieve the goals you have:

Momentum 1:

Momentum 2:

Momentum 3:

Daily Log

Write down what you did each day to build more momentum to create a snowball effect for your goals:

Day 1:

Day 2:

Day 3:

Day 4:

Day 5:

Day 6:

Day 7: *Rest and Reflect Day*

WEEK 44 GAME PLAN:
Keep Standing

#noslackjusthustle

"No matter how hard the challenge, or what the outcome is, you keep standing."

Nervous, scared, anxious… The young ballet dancer stood on stage waiting for the music to come on and begin her performance.

This is her first performance since she fell at competition and hurt her ankle. She debated no longer dancing because she felt embarrassed and wasn't sure she had the strength to do it again.

Her mom gave her continuous words of encouragement and told her a story of when she was a dancer and fell during a group performance. After telling the story, her mom finished with these two words for her daughter to remember, *"KEEP STANDING!"*

With the power of those words resonating in the mind of the young ballet dancer… she delivered her best performance to date! When she came off stage her mom was standing there, smiling with tears running down her cheeks. Her daughter gave her a hug and said, *"Thank you mom, I will always keep standing!"*

When things start to go bad, or we encounter a bad experience, it is the easiest time to walk away. Whether that be a sport, an extracurricular activity, a relationship, a job, or a business, rough times cause our minds to navigate towards a way out.

It is in these moments where we must look deeper and rediscover why we love what we do, love who we are with, or why we started this journey.

The powerful two words **KEEP STANDING** should filter into our minds. Challenges will always occur as we have addressed this many times throughout our journey. But we must realize, we have the power over the challenge, the challenge does NOT have the power over us.

No matter how difficult things may get or have been in the past, **KEEP STANDING!** You can and will achieve greatness, just... **KEEP... STANDING!**

Question for Thought

What area in your life do you need to think, "KEEP STANDING," to push forward and overcome the challenge?

Week 44 Take Action Game Plan Journal Entry

Write down the top three (3) things in your life that you sometimes debate doing or completing and you need to flip your mindset to KEEP STANDING:

Keep Standing 1:

Keep Standing 2:

Keep Standing 3:

Daily Log

Write down what you did each day to not give up and KEEP STANDING no matter how big or small the task or activity was:

Day 1:

Day 2:

Day 3:

Day 4:

Day 5:

Day 6:

Day 7: *Rest and Reflect Day*

WEEK 45 GAME PLAN:
Be Resourceful

#noslackjusthustle

"It's not all about having resources, it's about being resourceful!"

"Teacher, teacher!" cried out the student needing help on his assignment.

The teacher walked over and said to his student, *"What is it Jake?"*

"I don't know where to find the answer to this question,": responded Jake.

"Let's look at the question: What does the word 'experiment' mean?" said the teacher.

Jake looked at his teacher with a look on his face that displayed he had no idea. The teacher then said to the student, *"What resource could you use to discover your answer?"*

It was like an 'AHA' moment struck Jake! He responded loudly and firmly, *"The glossary!"*

The teacher looked at Jake with a smile on his face and said, *"Now that's the way to be resourceful!"*

Being resourceful is one of the most valuable things I could ever teach my children or students. As a parent and teacher, I always use this phrase with them: ***"Be Resourceful!"***

We live in a world where we have so many resources at our exposure, there is no excuse not to be resourceful. In the current time when writing this, we have so much information at our hands from internet articles to how-to videos that can teach us how to complete certain tasks we desire.

When I give out tests to my students, I allow them to use their notes, books, and the internet as a resource. My thought process is, if they know how to locate the resource to obtain the result or answer they want, then that is just as valuable as being the resource itself through studying and memorizing.

My encouragement to you is whether you are starting a business, working on an at-home task, or trying something new, be resourceful when trying to discover the answers or solutions you need.

Question for Thought

Have you already used resources to help you find solutions to any difficulties or problems you need to solve?

Week 45 Take Action Game Plan Journal Entry

Write down three (3) resources you could use to help you with a problem you need to solve:

Resource 1:

Resource 2:

Resource 3:

Daily Log

Write down each day what resources you used to help you find a solution you needed to a problem you had and how the resource helped you find this solution:

Day 1:

Day 2:

Day 3:

Day 4:

Day 5:

Day 6:

Day 7: *Rest and Reflect Day*

WEEK 46 GAME PLAN:
Start Bringing Value

#noslackjusthustle

"Bringing value will make the difference in your results."

YAWN! As the students in the class listen to the teacher, there are yawns and sighs of being tired and bored out of their minds. It's English Class, and Ms. Thomas is teaching the students about Old English literature. The bell rings and class is dismissed.

Discouraged, Miss Thomas goes home that evening struggling and wondering how to reach students. As she was listening to her nightly motivational video, she heard something about bringing value. She thought to herself, *"I have an idea..."* Excited... She started researching what she would implement for her lesson tomorrow.

As her students walk into class the next day, they have the same dismal looks on their faces. One student asked in a bored drawn out tone, *"What are we going to learn today, Ms. Thomas?"*

Ms. Thomas replied, *"We are continuing our journey with Old English."*

The class sighed, and some already put their heads down. Then all of a sudden, their favorite hip hop song came on the speaker as Ms. Thomas starts singing the lyrics along with the song. The kids' heads popped up from the desk and a new look of excitement came across their faces. Ms. Thomas' entire class started bumping to the beat! Now they had something that they valued and they were willing to learn how hip hop relates to Old English.

Value... we all place value on different things. What we value most is what we tend to focus on or pay attention to the most.

Look at the story above. The teacher is teaching the same concept both days, but the students start to pay attention when it is taught in a way that they enjoy and value.

It is imperative that if you want to see results in something you do, you must find value or display value to others. If you want to own a business, you need something of value for people to follow you, listen to you, or purchase from you, what you have created.

The more value that you bring to others, the more your results will increase.

Question for Thought

How will you start bringing value to others?

Week 46 Take Action Game Plan Journal Entry

Write down three (3) things that you can do to start bringing value to others at home, at work, or in your business:

Bringing Value 1:

Bringing Value 2:

Bringing Value 3:

Daily Log

Write down each day what you did to display value to others:

Day 1:

Day 2:

Day 3:

Day 4:

Day 5:

Day 6:

Day 7: *Rest and Reflect Day*

WEEK 47 GAME PLAN:
The Thanksgiving Challenge

#noslackjusthustle

"Take time to give thanks for all that you have."

The college student walked into his advisor's office for a meeting. They were discussing some of the things that were going on and the struggles the student was having in school. The advisor listened to every word the student said. After the student was finished the advisor responded asking if the student was thankful.

Unsure by what the advisor meant, the student asked, *"Thankful for what?"*

"Let me rephrase that. What are you thankful for?"

The student responded, *"I'm thankful for my family, my health, and the abilities I have."*

In reply, the advisor said, *"That's great! But now go back and think deeper. What should you really be grateful for? What about the toothbrush you used to brush your teeth this morning? What about the ability to wake up and be able to see? What about the bed sheets you have on your bed?"*

At that moment, the student's mouth dropped, and his eyes opened wide. He finally realized that he had a lot more to be thankful for than he had ever realized.

The advisor then challenged the student to go back to his dorm room and write down EVERY single thing he was thankful for on that day.

Wow! What an eye opener! Think about every little thing that you or I have, and we truly have a lot to be thankful for! If you didn't know, I was that college student. My advisor challenged me to do this, and it was one of the greatest challenges I have ever accepted in my life!

Now it's time for your challenge!

What I would like and encourage you to try is this same activity. **The Thanksgiving Challenge.** Get a few sheets of paper and write down EVERYTHING, and I mean EVERYTHING that you are thankful for! Go deeper than all of the big things you are thankful for, and think of every little thing you have been blessed with to be thankful for.

An attitude of true gratitude is an amazing thing.

Happy Thanksgiving and/or Happy Holidays to you and your family!

Question for Thought

*Did you complete **The Thanksgiving Challenge**?*

Week 47 Take Action Game Plan Journal Entry

Write down three (3) things you never realized before that you should be thankful for:

Thankful For 1:

Thankful For 2:

Thankful For 3:

Daily Log

Write down what you did each day to show the people in your life you are thankful for them:

Day 1:

Day 2:

Day 3:

Day 4:

Day 5:

Day 6:

Day 7: *Rest and Reflect Day*

WEEK 48 GAME PLAN:
Next Level Mindset

#noslackjusthustle

"Out work everyone and make time to get yourself to the next level."

"Five more, come on now, five more," shouted the coach.

"I can't coach, I'm too tired. I was up late last night," replied Joe, the team's star running back.

The coach blew the whistle and sent the team in to shower up as practice was over. The coach told Joe to stay behind so he could talk to him. Joe took a knee, but the coach instructed him to stand face-to-face and look him in the eye.

"Joe. Do you realize the potential you have? You have a shot at a scholarship, to go to the next level. You said this is something you dreamed of. The team looks up to you, and you are saying you can't do things because you were up late. I'm going to tell you this now Joe. You NEED to take your mindset to the next level if you want to get there. The only way you can achieve greatness is if you keep pushing and keep working towards that next level. If you want it, you have to out work everyone. You should be the first one to step foot on this field, and the last to leave. I believe in you son. But it's on you whether you take yourself to the next level or not. Now go in and get a shower."

Joe stayed standing there for a minute as the coach walked away. He realized he had a choice because he hadn't put forth all of the effort he could. For the next hour, he worked on his craft. The five more that Joe's coach asked for, now became fifty more. Joe was ready to implement a **NEXT LEVEL MINDSET.**

As we are weeks away from ending the start of our new journey, it is now time to up the game even more and develop a **NEXT LEVEL MINDSET!**

In whatever you do, work to perfect your craft. If you own a business, if you are a CEO, if you are an advisor, whatever it is you are, perfect that craft! The big question is, how do I do that?

I relate things to sports. Develop a **NEXT LEVEL MINDSET** and be the first to arrive and the last to leave. Set an example for everyone around you to be the best they can be.

For me, my **NEXT LEVEL MINDSET** starts in the home. I am the first one to wake up in my house and the last to go to bed. The reason I do this is to optimize time with my family, but then also get my ass to work for our family goals. The two (2) hours I am awake before my wife and kids awake, and the two (2) hours I stay awake after they go to bed is my grind time!

Those four (4) total hours are when I use my **NEXT LEVEL MINDSET** and get my workout in, work on my business, explore and learn more about how to improve my craft.

Find a way that works for you to implement the **NEXT LEVEL MINDSET** and let's make your goals and dreams a reality!

Question for Thought

*How will you start working towards and developing a **NEXT LEVEL MINDSET**?*

Week 48 Take Action Game Plan Journal Entry

*Write down three (3) things you will start doing to develop and implement a **NEXT LEVEL MINDSET**:*

NEXT LEVEL MINDSET 1:

NEXT LEVEL MINDSET 2:

NEXT LEVEL MINDSET 3:

Daily Log

*Write down what you did each day to start implementing a **NEXT LEVEL MINDSET!***

Day 1:

Day 2:

Day 3:

Day 4:

Day 5:

Day 6:

Day 7: *Rest and Reflect Day*

WEEK 49 GAME PLAN:
Prove Yourself Right

#noslackjusthustle

"Prove yourself right, you will prove others wrong in the process anyway."

It was the championship game to conclude the tournament. The head coach looked at his assistant coach Tom and said, *"How about we put Sam at shortstop this game."*

The assistant coach responded not knowing Sam was sitting close enough to hear, *"No coach. We want to win this game."*

Sam's mouth dropped from a smile to absolute devastation. After a few minutes went by, Sam began thinking to himself, *"I'll prove him wrong. He will never say that again."*

Every time Sam met a challenge, he found something, a reason, to prove someone or something wrong. It motivated him to be successful. But, as time rolled on and he got older he began to reflect. He was so focused on proving other people wrong, that he never focused on reaching the goals that he wanted to achieve.

Finally, Sam made the decision to no longer worry about what other people thought, and focus on proving himself right in reaching his goals. Now, he owns his own company worth millions of dollars and he focuses on donating to charities and helping others.

Have you ever been so focused on proving others wrong that you lost focus and sight of your own goals? Proving others wrong can be a great motivation, but is it the right motivation?

I built most of my life focusing on proving other people wrong. All this did was allow them to have more control over me than myself. When I changed my mindset to focusing on proving myself right, that's when the outside noise stopped mattering. That's when I gained control. It became all about my goals, what I wanted to accomplish, and what I believe I can do.

Don't give others leverage or control over you. Start taking control of yourself. Focus on proving yourself right. A bonus to proving yourself right is that in the process, you will prove others wrong anyway!

Question for Thought

How will you eliminate the distraction of others and focus on proving them wrong, and instead prove yourself right?

Week 49 Take Action Game Plan Journal Entry

Write down three (3) things or areas of life you need to prove yourself right in:

Prove Yourself Right 1:

Prove Yourself Right 2:

Prove Yourself Right 3:

Daily Log

Write down what you did each day to begin proving yourself right in an area of life that is important to you:

Day 1:

Day 2:

Day 3:

Day 4:

Day 5:

Day 6:

Day 7: *Rest and Reflect Day*

WEEK 50 GAME PLAN:
Every Second Counts

#noslackjusthustle

"Make every second you have now count! For you, for your family, and for what you love!"

The retired dad sat at the dining room table after his first son's high school graduation ceremony proud of what his son had accomplished.

His son looked sad and upset though. So the dad asked, *"What's wrong son?"*

The son responded with tears in his eyes, *"Dad… you missed my baseball games, you missed my high school musical, and you missed ALL of my elementary Christmas plays. Why dad? Why weren't you there?*

Stunned, the dad did not know how to respond. He knew that he missed all of those events due to work commitments and other time commitments. Now, his son has graduated, and he missed so many moments that were valuable to his son that he never recognized…

Let's be blunt here. You have one moment guaranteed in your life. That moment is **NOW**! Every second of every moment you have counts! What you do **NOW** begins molding your future. What you do **NOW** impacts you, your loved ones, and everything you do.

Ask yourself this question right now: *What matters to you most right **NOW**?*

Answer that question honestly. **NOW** is the perfect time to make every second count for what matters most to you!

Here is the math, there are 86,400 seconds in a day. That's 86,400 opportunities to do something great. 86,400 seconds to impact your family! 86,400 opportunities to make a difference! 86,400 opportunities to change a life! 86,400 opportunities to change your life! Use every second, make every second count, impact yourself, impact your family, and impact the world!

Question for Thought

You have the time (86,400 seconds a day), you have the opportunity (life), what will you commit to, to make it count?

Week 50 Take Action Game Plan Journal Entry

Write down three (3) things you will commit to each day to make every second count:

Commitment 1:

Commitment 2:

Commitment 3:

Daily Log

Write down what you did each day to make every second count:

Day 1:

Day 2:

Day 3:

Day 4:

Day 5:

Day 6:

Day 7: *Rest and Reflect Day*

WEEK 51 GAME PLAN:
A Christmas Story

#noslackjusthustle

"The greatest gift in life is life itself, enjoy and embrace every moment with those you love!"

The alarm went off. The couple awoke. Time to get ready for a new day. Christmas Eve to be exact! Stephanie and Scott were a young couple, married for a little over a year, full of ambition and very excited because Stephanie was 10-weeks pregnant. They were also blessed with the opportunity to drive with each other to work everyday. The young couple enjoyed their drives to start their day off together.

Done getting ready on this beautiful Christmas Eve morning, they began their drive to the office. Both excited that Christmas is one day away, and that this will be the last Christmas where it is only the two of them. Scott turns on his turn signal to get on the on-ramp to the six lane heavily populated highway they travel every morning. The couple's offices were in the city and this was the easiest and quickest way to travel there.

As the couple continued their drive, all of a sudden, the most unexpected thing occurred. Stephanie looked out the windshield during the drive and saw something out of the corner of her eye. She fully turned and looked to see a stray tire heading straight towards the car. The tire crossed three lanes of opposing traffic, a median strip, and two other lanes to get to Scott and Stephanie's car. In shock, Scott continued to drive, hoping to avoid the tire.

BOOM!!!!!

The tire hit the driver side door and the car spun out of control doing a 360 degree turn. The tire rolled off the road, damaging the car, and leaving it stalled out on the highway. Both Scott and Stephanie appeared to be okay, but the shock of the vehicle, and the other traveler involved, the baby!

An ambulance quickly arrived on the scene and immediately Scott and Stephanie were rushed to a local hospital, nervous and praying everything was okay with the baby. As the young couple arrived at the hospital, they continued hoping that a miracle would happen this Christmas, and the baby would be safe and healthy. Doctor Andrews entered the emergency room. He and his staff assessed Stephanie and scheduled an ultrasound to check on the baby. The couple could hear the clock ticking, but felt as if time had stopped.

Doctor Andrews began the ultrasound searching for the baby and the heartbeat. A minute went by... nothing. Two minutes gone... still nothing. Finally, the third minute and he was able to find the baby, and the heartbeat was strong! A Christmas prayer answered! The baby was safe! Scott and Stephanie were okay! A true blessing! The couple was overwhelmed with joy! Their lives and mindset now changed forever, fully understanding that the greatest gift in life is life itself!

As we are coming to a close with our journey together, my sincere hopes are that you have grown and developed your belief, your confidence, and your motivation to achieve the goals you have always wanted as well as realized how special life really is.

After you finish working through your action steps and your journal today, I encourage you, go give your loved ones a hug. Let them know how special they are to you. Then, reflect on how special they are and what they mean to you..

With a new week, new month, new year coming upon us soon, we have one more week to go!

Question for Thought

What did you take away from the story?

Week 51 Take Action Game Plan Journal Entry

Write down three (3) ways you will show your loved ones how special they are to you!

Special Showcase 1:

Special Showcase 2:

Special Showcase 3:

Daily Log

Write down what you did each day to show your loved ones that they are special to you:

Day 1:

Day 2:

Day 3:

Day 4:

Day 5:

Day 6:

Day 7: *Rest and Reflect Day*

WEEK 52 GAME PLAN:
Time To Take Action

#noslackjusthustle

"Time is limited. Don't lose out on your opportunity to live your dream. Take action NOW!"

"I want to start my own business to help people by..."

"I want to start a nonprofit focused on helping..."

"I want to create a scholarship program for..."

"I want to open a shelter for..."

"I want to write a book providing value about..."

"I want to invent..."

"I want to launch..."

As the young couple walked out of the cemetery from reading all of the tombstones, the gate read: ***"The BEST ideas that never were!"***

Do you feel the power of what that couple experienced?

Don't take your passions, your goals, or your dreams to the grave. You have the power to change what's written on the tombstone from *I want to...* to *I succeeded in...* Whatever is stopping you, whatever is holding you back, fight it. Don't lose out on the opportunity you have to live your dream because you chose not to take action.

As we conclude our journey together, my sincere hopes are that you have grown and developed your belief, your confidence, and your motivation to achieve the goals you have always wanted.

With a new opportunity now upon us, go and make this your time! Make your dreams and goals a reality! Take Action NOW and pursue your dreams today! God bless!

Question for Thought

What baggage holds you back from taking action on your dreams today?

Week 52 Take Action Game Plan Journal Entry

Write down the top three (3) baggages that hold you back from taking action on your dreams:

Baggage 1:

Baggage 2:

Baggage 3:

Daily Log

Write down what you will do each day to start taking action now and working towards your goals and dreams!

Day 1:

Day 2:

Day 3:

Day 4:

Day 5:

Day 6: *Today is the day where you release everything that is holding you back! Time to get rid of the baggage forever! On a piece of paper, I want you to draw the outline of a suitcase. (This does not have to be perfect, just symbolic of baggage!) Within the suitcase, write down the three (3) baggage claims you wrote for your Journal Entry this week. Now, play your favorite song that gets you motivated, pumped up, excited. Take your baggage claim paper with you outside, with the music playing, and in a safe manner burn it or throw it away! (If you have a firepit, throw it in the fire! If not, do this safely so you do not burn yourself. If you feel uncomfortable burning it, then open up a garbage bag, crumble the paper and throw your baggage away.) Now, your baggage is gone forever! Never look back again!*

Day 7: *Rest and Reflect Day*

A Final Thank You

#noslackjusthustle

"Always display an attitude of gratitude!"

Thank you to every person who took the time to read this book, join our social media group *(No Slack Just Hustle)*, subscribe to our channel, and support how we are trying to impact the world in a positive way! I enjoyed sharing some of my personal stories with you throughout this book, and I hope that they have helped you determine your path towards success!

I hope that this book inspired you to do great things and that you have learned how to develop a plan filled with passion to go into the world and do great things!

Please feel free to reach out on social media or message me if you ever need any help or have any questions. My handles are: @coachfic and @coachficsfootballacademy.

ALWAYS remember, YOU are special, YOU can make a difference, and ONE person really can impact the world in a positive way.

Go, be great, achieve your goals, and help make others see the greatness within them too!

And remember... in everything you do... NO SLACK, JUST HUSTLE!

God bless,

Coach Fic